The Art Of

Buddhism

The Hidden Truth To Be

Happy In Your Own Way

By

Sherman Evans

Table of Contents

Chapter 11: The Twelve Links Of Dependent Origination............93

Chapter 12: The Seven Factors 113

Chapter 13: The Foundation Of Mindfulness 121

Introduction

What is it that you want? Though I do not know you, I know the answer! Regardless of how you answer this question, your underlying desire is to be happy. You may disagree with this statement and say that what you want is love or more money. However, if you drill down deep enough, you will find that you have a belief that having love or more money will make you happy. This underlying intention drives everything that you do in life.

The challenge is that the happiness that we experience, should we get what we desire, exists only temporarily. Have you ever received anything in your life that brought you lasting joy, a happiness that is permanent? I would guess that the answer is "no."

The pursuit of happiness is made even more challenging in today's society. We live in a society that is experiencing rapid change. Whether it be economical, political, technological, or the environment, many of us have a sense of uncertainty for the future.

Having said all of this, I can tell you that there is an answer that addresses not just these challenges, but all difficulties. Yes, I claim *all* the problems! If my last statement leaves you suspicious, I do not blame you. I would be doubtful if such a claim was made to me 20 years ago.

Twenty years ago, I was highly educated, scientifically oriented, and a critical thinker. I also was searching for happiness. Today, I remain highly educated, scientifically oriented, and a critical thinker. However, one thing did change for me: I have enjoyed lasting happiness for the past 20 years!

That I achieved this sense of wellbeing may seem extraordinary; however, anyone could do the same.

I can confidently make all of these claims because I have learned that happiness is innate to our existence. There is no need to find happiness, as it is our natural state. The question is not how do we obtain it; instead, it is how do we see through the illusions that prevent us from experiencing it.

How I learned to see through my illusions was through studying Buddhism. I was introduced to Buddhism 20 years ago. Since then, I have practiced its teachings consistently. I have written this book because I want to share what I have learned so that others may benefit.

My intentions are not to persuade you to become Buddhist; instead, it is to share with you the principles that I have learned. These principles can be applied to your own life, regardless of your belief system. If you are looking for happiness, a sense of inner peace, greater compassion, to become more resilient, or to develop greater wisdom, the 2,500-year-old tradition of Buddhism may offer you what you are looking for!

Regardless of your religious beliefs, you have an opportunity to create significant changes in your life by learning from this ancient wisdom. Do not wait to get what you really want! Read this book, learn from it, and apply what you learn to your life. Let this book be your first step to achieving a life of unshakable happiness.

Chapter 1: The History Of Buddhism

The following is a brief overview of the history of Buddhism.

Where Did Buddhism Originate?

Buddhism originated in North East India. In the sixth century B.C. [1]., Prince Siddhartha became enlightened, after which he became known as Shakyamuni. Shakyamuni devoted his life to spreading his teachings as he traveled through India [2].

During the 3rd century B.C.E. [1], King Ashoka converted to Buddhism in response to his war-torn era. Determined to spread the Buddha's teachings, he sent monks to the surrounding regions so that they could propagate them.

With time, Buddhism spread beyond India and became established in Tibet, Nepal, Ceylon, Burma, Central Asia, China, Japan, and eventually the Western world. Today, Buddhism is practiced by 350 million people worldwide [1].

What Is Buddha?

The word "Buddha" is derived from the Sanskrit word "bodhi," which means wisdom. Thus, Buddha indicates one who has "awakened" or has become enlightened.

The Buddha was neither a god nor a prophet. Instead, he was a mortal man who became enlightened. This man was Siddhartha Gautama, born in Nepal 2,500 years ago [2]. Being awakened, he understood the mechanics of life at the most profound level.

The awakening that Siddhartha obtained was not a gift from the gods, as Buddhism does not believe in an external deity. Instead, Buddhism believes that every living being has an inherent Buddha-nature.

Becoming enlightened involves revealing it. For this reason, every person has the potential to become a Buddha by the mere fact that they exist! After achieving enlightenment, the Buddha spent the remaining 45 years [1] of his life offering his teachings to those who were open to receiving them.

The Buddha passed away in 483 B.C.E [1]. He was known by a variety of names, depending on the part of the world. His other titles include Shakaymuni, Siddhatta Gotama, Siddartha Gautama, and Gautama Buddha.

Who Was Siddhartha Gautama?

Siddhartha Gautama lived 2,500 years ago [2] in what is today known as Nepal. Born into a royal family, Siddhartha Gautama's father had hopes that his son would someday inherit the throne. For this reason, he discouraged Siddhartha from leaving the palace.

His parents did not want him to be exposed to poverty, disease, and other undesirable conditions that existed outside in the community.

To encourage him to stay in the palace, his parents showered him with gifts and provided him a life of luxury. At age 29 [2], Prince Siddhartha left the palace and saw first hand what his father had tried so hard to protect him from.

Siddhartha saw people who were infirmed, who were ill, and he saw a corpse. Siddhartha later learned that everyone, at some point in their life, experiences these sufferings. Siddhartha realized that the people that he loved, his family, would eventually experience these sufferings as well. Because of this, he became determined to find a way to relieve suffering.

Siddhartha left his family and spent the next six years wandering through the forests, where he studied under various teachers and lived a life of an ascetic. Despite his ability to excel in the different spiritual practices that he was mentored in, Siddhartha remained dissatisfied. He still did not know how to relieve suffering.

Still determined to find his answer, Siddharta discarded all of the teachings that he learned and sat down under a Bodi tree and meditated. He refused to leave his spot until he found the answer for relieving humanity of its suffering. It was during this time that Siddhartha became enlightened. He would forever be known as the Buddha.

Upon achieving enlightenment, the Buddha created his teachings so that others may overcome suffering. He referred to his teachings as Dhamma-Vinaya [5], which may be translated to "The doctrine of discipline." The teachings provide a framework for developing an understanding of the workings of life. It is from Dhamma-Vinaya that the term dharma was derived.

What Are The Three Main Branches Of Buddhism?

The three main branches of Buddhism are Theravada, Mahayana, and Vajrayana. The following is a brief overview of these sects.

Theravada Buddhism

One of the oldest of the Buddhist sects, Theravada, observes a monastic tradition and follows orthodox teachings. The teachings focus on meditation, ethical conduct, and the cultivation of wisdom and insight.

Mahayana Buddhism

Unlike Theravada, Mahayana Buddhism adapts itself to the culture and times. For example, it is just as acceptable to sit in a chair when meditating as it is on the floor. Additionally, Mahayana places a greater emphasis on rituals than Theravada [9]. In the Mahayana tradition, it is believed that every sentient being possesses an enlightened nature within them. Additionally, the pursuit of awakening must involve working for the happiness of others.

Vajrayana

Vajrayana (Sanskrit for "Way of the diamond") Buddhism is related to Mahayana Buddhism and is founded on a complex system of beliefs that provide a path to awakening. Vajrayana Buddhism originated in India but then spread to the Himalayas. It is for this reason that Vajrayana Buddhism and Tibetan Buddhism share some overlap.

Chapter 2: Theravada Buddhism

Considered to be the oldest branch of Buddhism, Theravada Buddhism is most aligned with the original teachings of the Buddha. It is for this reason that it is referred to as the "Doctrine of the Elders" [4].

In Theravada, there is a focus on developing insight through the application of meditation, critical analysis, and experience as opposed to blind faith. It follows the scriptures contained in the Tipitaka or Pali canon.

Scholars consider these scriptures to be the oldest of the Buddhist teachings. The teachings of Theravada, such as the canonical, are written in Pali. A dialect of Middle Indo-Aryan, Pali was the spoken language at the time of the Buddha [4].

Where Is It Practiced?

Historically, Theravada Buddhism has been the dominant religion in Southeast Asia and Sri Lanka. In Thailand, there is a branch of Theravada Buddhism known as ThaiForest.

In the late 19th century, Theravada was introduced to the West. Since then, the popularity of Theravada has grown. Dozens of Theravada monasteries appeared in North America and Europe. Besides monasteries, numerous mediation centers were established throughout the West. Worldwide, 100 million people practice Theravada Buddhism [5].

History And Background Of The Religion

The origins of Theravada are derived from Vibbajjavada, a Buddhist sect that existed in Sri Lanka, around 3rd century B.C.E. In contrast, Mahayana Buddhism did not appear until the early first millennium C.E [5]. Theravada Buddhism follows the original monastic lifestyle, practices, and teachings as taught by the Buddha.

Theravada differs from other Buddhist sects in some ways. There is little sectarian division as compared to other Buddhist sects, Mahayana in particular. As a result, there is little or no difference in doctrines from one temple to the next [4].

As Buddhism spread across India, different sects of the religion were formed, with each of the factions interpreting the Buddha's teachings differently. One of these sects was the Mahayana sect, which was born from a reformed interpretation of the teachings [4].

The Mahayana sect came to be known as the "Greater Vehicle," and it viewed other factions as being less authentic to the Buddha's original teachings. As a result, it referred to the other denominations, such as Theravada, as "Lesser Vehicle."

The Language Of Theravada

The Buddha died around 480 BCE [5]. His cousin Ven. Ananda, with the help of his assistant, had committed the Buddha's sermons to memory. They had become the living repository of 45 years worth of sermons.

The Buddha's teachings were passed down orally until 250 BCE [5] when a group of senior monks systematically arranged the sermons (which were known as Suttas) and put them down into writing. The writings were organized into three groups, the Vinaya Pitaka, Sutta Pitaka, and the Abhidhamma Pitaka. These three groups were known collectively as the Tipitaka [5].

The Tipitaka was translated into Pali at the start of the fifth century BCE [5]. The Tipitaka, along with the canonical texts, became the totality of classical

Theravada scripture. Mahayana sutras are not considered valid by Theravada because they are written in Sanskrit instead of Pali.

Beliefs Of Enlightenment

The ultimate purpose behind all Buddhist sects is finding enlightenment. In general, views regarding awakening are similar among the various factions; however, Theravada's perspective of enlightenment does have some differences with other sects.

In Pali, the term Arhat refers to one who has achieved awakening. To be enlightened is to free oneself of the cycle of birth and death. Becoming an Arhat is solely the result of the individual's effort.

In contrast, the Mahayana faith believes enlightenment is an inherent potential that is found in all people. Because of this, one reaches awakening by working to help others find it as well. The concept of Bodhisattva embodies this belief.

Just one level under Buddhahood, the Bodhisattva uses the wisdom that they gained to work for the happiness of others. In Theravada, the pursuit of enlightenment is carried out within a monastic lifestyle.

A core practice in Theravada is meditation, and Vipassana meditation is used to reach awakening. In Vipassana meditation, one develops mental discipline and insight into the nature of the self by observing the interconnectedness of the mind and body. While meditation is performed in Mahayana Buddhism, not all of its sects practice it.

Chapter 3: Mahayana Buddhism

As Buddhism spread throughout India and beyond, some sects became more popular with the local people than others. In this regard, Mahayana stands out in the history of Buddhism [8].

Mahayana originated in Northern India and became the most popular form of Buddhism in Asia, Korea, China, and Japan. Mahayana Buddhism is an "umbrella religion" in that it is comprised of a wide range of Buddhist sects and belief systems. It is this diversity of teachings that led Mahayana Buddhism to become known as the "Greater Vehicle [8]."

Practitioners of Mahayana Buddhism focus on developing compassion and insight. In contrast, Theravada Buddhism focuses on developing conduct, mental discipline, and wisdom.

The Ten Worlds

In certain sects of Mahayana Buddhism, there is a model that depicts the various potential life states that are found in a person. These life states are referred to as "worlds." They are hell, hungry spirits, animals, asuras, human beings, voice-hearers, cause-awakened ones, bodhisattvas, and Buddhahood.

Hell

Hell is the first and lowest world. When in the state of hell, we feel that we have no power and are unable to rise above our circumstances.

Hunger

Having an insatiable desire is the characteristic of the world of hunger, which is the second-lowest world. Such a person is continuously trying to fill a spiritual void within themselves.

Animals

In the world of animals, moral or ethical judgment takes a backseat to impulsiveness and immediate gratification. These three worlds are known as the three evil paths as they lead to suffering.

Asuras

The world of asuras is the fourth realm. It is characterized by anger. In this world, the person is obsessed with a sense of self-importance and appearing superior to others. They will conceal their true feelings to ingratiate themselves with others.

Human Beings

The fifth realm is the world of human beings. This life state is characterized by calmness, composure, and being humane to others. Despite the admirable qualities of this world, maintaining these qualities requires consistent effort.

Rapture

Feelings of rapture or joy are found in the world of heavenly beings. However, these feelings are transitory and can vanish with changes in circumstances or loss.

The six worlds just described are known as the six paths. These paths are unstable as they are easily influenced by external conditions. They cannot lead to self-mastery or real freedom. It is the goal of Buddhist practice to transcend the six paths so that one can enjoy a happiness that is self-determined.

Voice-Hearers

The world of voice-hearers is the first world that departs from the six paths. This is a world where the individual has reached partial awakening as a result of hearing the Buddha's teachings.

Cause Awakened One

The next highest world is that of the cause-awakened one. This individual achieves partial awakening through their own efforts, contemplations, and observations.

The partial awakening that is reached by the Voice Hear and Cause Awakened One arises from understanding the principles of cause and effect, the impermanence of all phenomena, and the letting go of attachments. Such knowledge leads to liberation.

Bodhisattvas

The ninth world is that of the bodhisattvas. In this state, the individual has made a determination to obtain full awakening. We will discuss the bodhisattvas in more detail later in this chapter.

Buddhahood

The tenth and highest world is that of Buddhahood. At this state of life, there is a recognition that all beings are the manifestation of the supreme universal law. Further, there is an understanding that this supreme law is inherent within the life of all beings. This is a world that is impossible to describe in words. The best that can be said is that it is a life state of eternal happiness and freedom.

The Ten Worlds are found within every person, and they are mutually inclusive of each other. In any given world, the other nine worlds are found within it. Each person has a world or worlds that are dominant for them. They can switch from world to world numerous times on any given day. Buddhist practice provides the practitioner with the ability to move toward the higher worlds and make them their dominant life state, with the ultimate goal of attaining Buddhahood.

Bodhisattva

As previously noted, the development of compassion and insight is the focus of Mahayana Buddhism. The one who is a Bodhisattva dedicates their lives to the service of others. One cannot achieve liberation with a self-interest orientation. For this reason, to obtain enlightenment requires one to serve others by teaching them how to overcome suffering.

The appearance of the Bodhisattva in Buddhist philosophy had significant implications for social change. It opened up the practice to ordinary people, who did not want to renounce their life to become monks or nuns. Additionally, women could become Bodhisattvas. It is for this reason that the Bodhisattva became a crucial element in the success of Mahayana Buddhism spreading [8].

Chapter 4: Vajrayana Buddhism

A version of Tantric Buddhism, Vajrayana Buddhism originated in India and spread to neighboring countries. It has become the predominant religion in Tibet, Nepal, Mongolia, and Bhutan [11].

Gaining Insight From Within

Vajrayana Buddhism is also known as Mantrayana Buddhism. Mantrayana translates to "Vehicle of the Mantra, "referring to the recitation of mantras. Mantras are useful during meditation as they improve concentration by preventing one's mind from wandering. By doing so, the practitioner can focus their attention on their experience of reality.

In the *Quintessence of the Union of Mahamudra and Dzogchen* [11], there is a song that includes the following verses:

The View of Vajrayana

The essence of the mind of all beings

Is primordially the essence of Buddhahood.

Its empty essence is the birthless dharmakaya.

*Its clear, distinct appearances are the
sambhogakaya.*

*Its unceasing compassion is the variegated
nirmanakaya.*

*The inseparable union of those three is the
svabhavikakaya.*

Its eternal changelessness is the mahasukhakaya.

The messages behind these verses are as follows:

The mind of all sentient beings, regardless of its clarity, is the Buddha. It has been so from the beginning of time. Further, the mind of every being is inherently aware and perfect.

Being inherently aware and perfect is the mind's very nature. The mind is free of all deficiencies and contains all qualities. It for this reason that the mind is called Buddha.

Even when our minds are confused or wander (samsara), even when awakening is attained, the mind's essential nature remains untouched.

According to the Tantric view, enlightenment is the understanding that principles, which are seemingly opposite to each other, are two sides of the same coin. The mind exhibits both non-existence and existence. No one has ever seen a mind; yet, the properties of the mind cannot be denied.

Thoughts, perceptions, and sensations all arise from the mind. Everything that we experience presents itself to us as a thought, perception, or sensation (perceptions include the perception of images, sounds, smells, and tastes). Because of this, all that we experience arises from the mind. To understand this experientially, as opposed to intellectually, is to be awakened.

The song continues as follows:

This primordial innate presence in yourself

Was not created by the compassion of the buddhas, by the blessing of the gurus,

Or by the profound special essentials of the dharma.

Wisdom has primordially been present in this way.

All sutras and tantras are in accord on this.

The meaning of these verses is as follows:

There is an ageless presence within each of us. This presence is inherent to our being and is eternal. This presence is untainted by any experience, and it transcends any experience. Further, we can't be separated from it. Neither born or created, this presence is the stratum for all of life. It is from it that wisdom flows.

These two passages refer to the mind. For those of us who are from the West, this teaching can be made more easily understood if we replace the word "mind" with "awareness."

The following is an exercise that will allow you to catch a glimpse of what these passages are speaking of. Note: When doing this exercise, do not resort to your knowledge or past experiences. Instead, you rely only on your immediate experience.

Exercise

1. Select an object in your environment.

2. When you have selected an object, observe it. As you watch it, determine for yourself if seeing comes to an end at a certain point, at which point the object begins. Or, does the act of seeing and the object being seen flow into each other?

3. Next, ask yourself if seeing takes place from within you, or does it take place from outside of you.

4. Now ask yourself, how do you know seeing is taking place? You know that you are seeing because you are aware of it!

5. Finally, ask yourself if the awareness of seeing ends at a certain point, at which point seeing begins. Or, does the awareness of seeing and the act of seeing flow into each other.

This exercise may take practice before you can develop the acuity to discern the answers. When you have developed this level of acuity, you will realize the following:

- The act of seeing and the object being seen are inseparable from each other.

- Seeing takes place from within you.
- The awareness of seeing and the act of seeing are inseparable.

From these findings, we can conclude that the object being seen, the act of seeing, the one that is doing the seeing, and the awareness of seeing are inseparable from each other. Further, we can conclude that the object being seen, the act of seeing, and you (the one who is doing the seeing) are all found within awareness. Awareness is constant, while the experiences that we are aware of are continually changing.

There has never been a time when you have not been aware. You are aware of your thoughts, your perceptions, and your sensations. You are aware of the waking state and when you are asleep. There is an awareness of whether you are dreaming or not. You have an awareness of memory and the lack of memory, confusion, and clarity. Even more profound, you are aware of your own existence!

Everything that you experience occurs in awareness. Without awareness, there can be no experience. Awareness is without color, form, shape, or size. It is void of all qualities; yet, all of the experience arises from it. Awareness (also known as consciousness) is what Buddhist teachings refer to as mind and mind is Buddha.

Chapter 5: Buddhism And Other Religions

Though Buddhism is commonly seen as being a religion, it lacks many of the characteristics typically associated with a religion. Here are just a few examples [16]:

- Buddhism does not believe in an external deity; there are no gods in Buddhism.
- Buddhism was founded by the original Buddha, a mortal man.
- Buddhism lacks any dogma.
- Buddhism does not require its adherents to have blind faith.
- Nowhere in Buddhism is sin referenced.
- Buddhism does not have a creation story.
- The concept of a soul is not found in Buddhism.
- The Buddha was not a savior, and he made this clear to his followers. Instead, he was a teacher.
- In Buddhism, the practitioner is taught to balance compassion, faith, and logic.

Secular Buddhism

While the teachings of many Buddhist sects delve into the metaphysical (i.e., reincarnation and other realms), secular Buddhist embrace the core teachings of the Buddha and disregard any metaphysical aspects of the teachings [14].

Secular Buddhist view Buddhism through the lens of rationality and humanism. Rather than dedicating their life to reaching Nirvana, secular Buddhists use the core ethical teachings, such as the Eightfold Path, to enhance human life through daily efforts.

The secular approach to Buddhism is about action, not belief. When the core teachings, such as the Four Noble Truths, are put into action, what one believes is irrelevant as it is the final outcome of the action taken that determines if the teachings are true or not.

Buddhism's Place Among The World Religions

While Buddhism does not fit within the traditional structures associated with a religion, most people still regard it as one. It is from this context that we will now briefly explore the similarities and differences between Buddhism and other religions.

Buddhism And Christianity

The following is a brief comparison of Buddhist and Christain belief systems.

Life After Death

Buddhism believes in rebirth, which means we are caught in an endless cycle of being born, dying, and being reborn again. Suffering is an inherent part of this cycle. The attainment of Nirvana breaks this cycle and liberates one from suffering.

Additionally, Buddhism does not believe in the soul. Traditionally, most Christians believe the soul goes to heaven, where we encounter God and our deceased loved ones. Different Buddhist sects may differ in their beliefs of what it takes to get into heaven. Some Christians believe in hell, which is the destination of unrepentant sinners [16].

The Nature Of Humans

In Buddhism, ignorance is the nature of human beings. The ignorance that is being referred to is the ignorance of our fundamental nature, which is Buddha or enlightenment. In Christianity, man's nature is that of sin, which was inherited from Adam.

Based on this perspective, humans need to have their sins forgiven by God. Sin is a concept that is not found in Buddhism [16].

Salvation

In Buddhism, salvation is the result of achieving awakening or Nirvana. This is accomplished by disciplining the mind and cultivating wisdom. In Christianity, salvation is through Christ.

Buddhism And Hinduism

The following is a brief comparison of Buddhism and Hinduism belief systems.

Philosophy

Buddhism and Hinduism share common beliefs regarding rebirth and the cycle of birth and death. Both religions also share the belief that liberation comes from breaking this cycle. Both believe that attachment to the world of form, including thoughts, leads to suffering. For this reason, both religions teach that one must learn to anchor themselves in their inner silence, rather than their outer world. It is for this reason that both religions place great emphasis on meditation [17].

Theology

Buddhism does not believe in gods or deities, while Hinduism has a plethora of gods. While both religions believe in the Buddha, Hinduism believes the Buddha is the incarnation of the God Vishnu. Buddhists, on the other hand, believe that the Buddha was a mortal being [17].

Buddhism And Islam

The following is a brief comparison of the beliefs found in Buddhism and Islam.

Life After Death

One of the core beliefs in Buddhism is rebirth, that every sentient being undergoes a continuous cycle of birth, death, and being reborn again. A central goal in Buddhism is to break this cycle, which is Nirvana. In Islam, all beings that can reason are accountable to an all-mighty God. On judgment day, they will be rewarded for their good deeds and punished for their evil ones.

The Nature Of Humans

In Buddhism, ignorance is the basic nature of human beings. This ignorance is the lack of knowledge for the truth of who we are at the most fundamental level. Our essential being, which is the Buddha or enlightenment, is concealed by the workings of our mind.

In Islam, it is believed that humans are pure and innocent at birth. When reaching adolescence, we are responsible for our actions and the decisions that we make. In Islam, faith and action are the same, a belief that is shared by Buddhism as well [18].

Sin

Buddhism has no notion of sin. In Islam, anything

that strays from the norms of the religion is considered to be a sin. To go against religious norms is to go against Allah. Ultimate forgiveness can only come from God [18].

Marriage

In Buddhism, there are no expectations for marriage. The exception is for nuns and monks; they do not marry. The Buddha gave a discourse on the subject of marriage. He did not define marriage and left it open to reflect the norm of the culture and time. The Buddha stressed the importance of faithfulness and that it was inappropriate for men to marry women who were much younger than them [19].

Buddhism And Taoism

The following is a brief comparison of beliefs that are found in Buddhism and Taoism.

Founders Of The Religion

While Buddhism originated in India, Taoism has its roots in China. Lao Tzu founded Taoism, while the Buddha started Buddhism [19].

Beliefs In God

As with Buddhism, Taoism does not believe in a god or external deity. Instead, Taoism believes in a dynamic existence that consists of opposing forces. It is the relationship between these forces from which all phenomenal existence is created. For this reason, Tao's view of reality is similar to Buddhism, which believes that there is an innate wisdom that is the substrate of all existence and permeates all of life.

Life After Death

While Buddhism believes in rebirth, Taoism believes that all sentient and non-sentient beings are continuously evolving as they manifest in different forms. This evolving is based on past conduct. What this evolving is leading to is immortality. In this sense, Taoism is similar to Buddhism.

The Nature Of Humans

Buddhism believes the essential nature of humans is ignorance. Taoism believes that if we are aligned with the Tao, our suffering will cease, and we will experience immortality.

Beliefs About The Buddha

In Buddhism, the Buddha is seen as the foremost of all sages. In Taoism, the Buddha is believed to be a student of Lazo Tzu. Other than this, Taoism follows Buddhist teachings [19].

Gender Equality

In both religions, men and women are seen as being equal.

Attitudes Toward Other Religions

Both Buddhism and Taoism are accepting of other religions. As Buddhism is based on practical philosophy, it has a neutral approach toward other faiths.

Buddhism And Judaism

The following is a brief comparison of beliefs between Buddhism and Judaism.

God

Buddhism does not believe in the existence of a god. Judaism is monotheistic, meaning the belief in a single god.

Belief Systems

Buddhism observes the principles and precepts that are found in the various sutras. Judaism has the Ten Commandments. Some of the commandments include *Thou shalt not kill*, or *Thou shalt bear false witness against thy neighbor*.

Both Buddhism and Judaism believe that we, as individuals, are solely responsible for our inner spiritual growth and happiness. Buddhism believes in karma and practicing the Noble Eightfold Path, which includes codes of conduct such right view, right speech, and right actions. Similarly, Judaism believes that happiness and suffering are the product of our cumulative thoughts, words, and actions.

Incorporating Buddhism By Those Of Other Faiths

Because Buddhism's unique characteristics, those of other faiths can follow Buddhist philosophies while retaining their existing faith. Those of the Jewish religion is an example of this. A growing number of Jews are adopting Buddhist beliefs and practices [13].

There is a segment of Jews who have nontheistic beliefs. They often find Buddhism does a better job of meeting their spiritual needs without having to compromise their existing beliefs [13]. This is illustrated by the fact that meditation and mindfulness comprise a large part of Buddhism, practices that have universal appeal.

Chapter 6: Benefits Of Buddhism

Science has recently taken an interest in meditation. Once considered as being unworthy of study, meditation is now increasingly becoming a subject of research.

Rewiring The Brain

Interest in contemplative practice training has become increasingly mainstream, partly due to the discovery of neuroplasticity. Traditionally, the brain was believed to become fixed in its structure and function upon reaching a certain age.

Upon reaching a critical age, it was thought that new neuro-connections could not be made. Since then, research has demonstrated that the brain is not fixed, that it shows the potential of developing new neuro-connections even at advanced ages. This new view of the brain has led to greater interest in contemplative practice research, which has substantiated its benefits [26].

Elevating Emotions And Moods

The following are a few examples of research on how mediation and mindfulness affect emotions and moods.

1. Brain scans have revealed that the brains of those who regularly engage in contemplative practices showed a change in brain density. This increased density occurred in the parts of the brain that are associated with attention skills, memory, learning, empathy, and emotion regulation [21].

2. In studies conducted on prison populations, those inmates that practiced meditation demonstrated a reduction in anger and mood disturbances, assisting them in their rehabilitation and reintegration in society. Contemplative practices have also been

associated with a decrease in Post-Traumatic Stress Disorder symptoms in veterans [21].

Physical Benefits

The benefits of contemplative practice go beyond that of the mind; they are also physical. The following are comments on the benefits of contemplative practices as determined by research:

Benefits To The Blood

Performing contemplative practices can increase antibiotic levels in the blood while reducing the stress hormone cortisol and blood pressure [22]. Further, these benefits can appear after practicing contemplative practices for just twenty minutes a day for five days [22].

Meditation And Pain Reduction

A 2011 study found that contemplative practices can reduce the experience of pain. The study involved participants who were exposed to painful stimuli both before and after an 80-minute contemplative practice training.

Over half of the participants reported that their experience of pain, during the post contemplative practices training testing, was less intense or more tolerable. Magnetic resonance imaging (MRI) of the participants' brains revealed significant changes in their brains as a result of their involvement in contemplative practice [23].

Benefits To Nerve Cells

The University of Oregon concluded that meditation can cause changes in the brain that make it more resistant to acquiring mental illness. The conclusions were based on how contemplative practices increase the protective covering of nerve cells, known as myelin [25].

A Boost To Cancer Patients

Studies have concluded that contemplative practices can reduce stress-related symptoms of patients with breast cancer [30].

Improved Health In The Elderly

Researchers found that contemplative practice raised the health of their elderly participants by decreasing the gene expression that is associated with inflammation [26].

Benefits During Pregnancy

The results of a study by the University of Michigan revealed that pregnant women who meditated showed lower rates of depression as compared to those who did not practice [27].

Meditation And Weight Loss

Contemplative practices were a recommended component for weight loss programs, as expressed by seven out of 10 psychologists who participated in a survey by Consumer Reports and the American Psychological Association [29].

Meditation As A Sleep Aid

A University of Utah study found that contemplative practice training helped its participants improve their sleep habits. Participants reported getting a better night's sleep, which may be due to the increased control of their emotions and moods [24].

Chapter 7: Basic Practices And Benefits

The following are some principles found in Buddhist philosophy.

The Nature Of Reality

When sunlight shines on a rock, the light and the rock appear to be one. If the rock is removed, the light remains. Consciousness is like the sunlight, and experience is like the rock. Consciousness (awareness) is inseparable from that which is being experienced, yet it is independent of experience.

There can be no experience without the perceiving of it; yet, consciousness can exist without experience. Deep sleep is the stage of sleep when dreaming does not occur. At this stage, all that exists is pure awareness. It is referred to as pure awareness because it is free of experience.

Consciousness and experience are not two separate things. Instead, experience is an expression of consciousness. It is for these reasons that Buddhists say that everything that exists arises from the mind. Reality is neither fixed or objective. Instead, it is a projection of the mind. Reality is fluid and continually changing.

Anatta

Anatman is a core concept in Buddhist philosophy and refers to the fundamental nature of the self. The English translation of Anatman is "no-self." The Buddha taught that there is no permanent aspect of our existence [31].

The Buddha rejected the notion of a permanent self or soul. He believed the nature of a human being was no different than the rest of the phenomenal world. Our life is also transitory and continuously changing

[31].

Buddhism believes that our life is a composite of the five aggregates. The five aggregates are the body, sensations, perceptions, mental formations, and consciousness. It is our attachment to the five aggregates that lead to suffering. The purpose of Buddhist practice is to transcend this attachment. This transcendence is the mark of enlightenment or Nirvana.

Karma

The term "karma" is often used within spiritual circles and has become part of our lexicon. In Theravada Buddhism, karma is a significant part of its teachings. Karma refers to the law of cause and effect. We create causes through our thoughts, words, and deeds. Every thought, word, or deed is a cause that is set into motion. In turn, the cause elicits an effect of like kind.

Karma is comprised of three components: Desire, action, and memory. These three components create a feedback loop. Imagine a person is walking down the street and passes a bakery. The person detects a pleasant smell. In response to the scent, desire is experienced. The person enters the bakery and purchases the pastries, which is a form of action. When the person eats the cakes, memory is created (or reinforced). In turn, memory results in future desires.

Meditation And Mindfulness

There is so much overlap between mindfulness and meditation that attempting to distinguish between the two in this book would risk causing confusion. Generally speaking, mindfulness involves the knowledge of what is happening at the moment while meditation is about concentrating one's attention on an object.

What is most important to know is that both of these practices are wonderful tools for developing the level of consciousness that is needed to discern between our authentic nature and the five aggregates.

Applying What You Have Learned: Meditation And Karma Exercises

Meditation

When learning to meditate, it is important to understand some basic guidelines. If you do this, you will more likely enjoy your experience:

- Have an attitude of total acceptance of whatever you experience. Do not judge or resist anything.

- Do not try to change what you are experiencing.

- Allow everything that you experience to express itself freely

- Though you may become distracted by your thoughts, do not give in to them. Thoughts lack any power of their own. Instead, they gain their power from the attention that we give them.

The following are the steps for performing breath meditation, one of the simplest meditations. It is also fundamental to learn before attempting other forms of meditation.

1. Sit down in a comfortable position, close your eyes, and breathe normally.
2. Place your attention on your breath by focusing on the sensations of it traveling in and out of your body.
3. As your focus on your breath, you will experience the appearance of thoughts. When they appear, simply ignore them and return your attention back to your breath.
4. If you keep your focus on your breath, there will come a point when you can maintain your attention to it without any effort.

Karma

As a quick review, karma is action. In this case, action refers to setting something into motion. Our thoughts, words, and deeds are all causes that are set into motion. The effect of these causes is our karma. The following are two methods for evaluating your decisions before taking action on them.

Reflection

Ask yourself, what will be the consequences of the decision that you are about to make? When reflecting on the answers to this question, consider all stakeholders who will be affected by your decision. Your goal should be to make decisions that will benefit all those involved.

Meditation

The following meditation can help you in decision making:

1. Sit down in a comfortable position and close your eyes.

2. Pay attention to the flow of your breath as you follow it during inhalation and exhalation. Feel it as it courses through your body. Allow yourself to relax.

3. Think of a decision that you need to make. If you currently do not have a decision to make, create one that is relevant to you.

4. Next, think of the different options that you have when making your decision.

5. Now that you have considered your options, think of what the potential consequences for each option would be, if you decided to go with it . For example, if I had to make a decision on whether to buy a new car, I would consider the potential consequence for each option I am considering. What would be the consequences if I bought the car? What would be the consequences if I saved my money instead and used ride-sharing?

When doing this part of the meditation, do not over-analyze the situation. Instead, pay attention to the thoughts that come to you. This is not intended to be an intellectual exercise.

6. Now return your attention to your breath and allow yourself to relax. Do not engage with any of your thoughts; allow yourself to become relaxed and still within.

7. Now, while remaining in your peacefulness, I want you to review your options, one by one. Consider each option separately, giving it your full attention.

8. As you review the choice, ask yourself, "Should I say 'yes' or 'no' to this option?" When you do this, pay close attention to what you experience in the body.

9. When you think of this option, do you feel constricted or relaxed? Is your breathing relaxed or shallow? Does your chest feel hard or soft? Does your body feel stiff or tingly? Notice the sensations of the body and the quality of your breathing as you reflect on each option.

10. Without exception, you were intended to be happy in this life. Happiness is your birthright. Which option brings you the greatest sense of peacefulness in your body? Which option brings about the greatest ease in your breathing? Regardless of what your mind or conventional wisdom says, that is the option that is right for you.

If you had difficulty experiencing the sensations of the body as you consider your choices, please practice this meditation until you are able to do so.

Chapter 8: Four Noble Truths

From the Tipitaka comes one of the core teaching reaching enlightenment, the Four Noble Truths. The Four Noble Truths provide a blueprint to the reaching of enlightenment through a four-step process. This process is grounded in one's direct experience as opposed to belief or religious dogma. The process for awakening mirrors that of one who is trying to cure an illness.

A sick person experiences suffering or discomfort. To achieve good health, the person first must determine the nature of the illness. What are the symptoms created by the disease? When the symptoms are identified, a diagnosis must be made. When a diagnosis has been made, the final step is to cure the illness by applying an effective remedy.

In this case, the disease is suffering. The Four Noble Truths are as follows:

First Noble Truth (The nature of suffering): Suffering exists in both subtle and pronounced forms and is an inherent aspect of life.

Second Noble Truth (The source of suffering): Suffering is created by desire and ignorance of our fundamental nature.

Third Noble Truth (The cessation of Suffering): Freedom from suffering is available to all of us through clear perception and an enlightened mind.

Fourth Noble Path (The Path): Suffering can be eliminated by following the Four Noble Truths.

The First Noble Path

Just as a doctor must understand a patient's illness

before the patient can be treated, it is equally important to understand suffering before there can be freedom from it.

Suffering can occur in subtle or pronounced forms. Feelings of being dissatisfied or worried are subtle forms of suffering. Mourning the death of a loved one or experiencing severe depression are examples of pronounced suffering.

We know when we are happy or suffering; however, what most of us do not know is that happiness and suffering are not opposites. Instead, the seeds of suffering are found in happiness. This can be illustrated in the following scenario:

After working hard and saving his money, Fred buys his dream car, a Jaguar. Because he is now a proud owner of the vehicle, he is delighted. The next day, Fred drives his car to work, but he parks illegally on the street. When work is over, he returns to the car to find that he has received a ticket. Fred is now irritatcd, a subtle form of suffering.

As time goes on, Fred experiences financial challenges. As a result, he falls behind on his payments for his car loan. One morning, he wakes up to find that his car has been repossessed. Fred is now furious. Fred's subtle suffering is now pronounced suffering.

Most of us experience a similar dynamic. A situation or event occurs in our life, which makes us feel happy. However, that happiness begins to erode as our circumstances change. A core Buddhist belief is the nature of impermanence. Nothing in life is permanent. Everything that we experience is transitory or impermanent. Because of this, inherent within happiness is the potential for suffering.

When suffering expresses itself, it frequently starts off as subtle suffering. Subtle suffering may evolve into pronounced suffering. However, suffering, like everything else, is also impermanent. Because of this, suffering can turn into happiness. Suffering is born from the impermanence of happiness, while happiness arises from the transitory nature of suffering.

Second Noble Truth

The Buddhist term "interdependent origination" refers to how everything that exists arises from something else. The root cause of suffering is karma and negative emotions [32].

As indicated before, karma is action, be it in the form of our thoughts, words, or actions. Suffering does not come from outside of us; it originates from within us. We can not control the world around us. As long as we believe that our suffering is the result of what happens to us, we will never be able to overcome our suffering.

Fred attributed his happiness to the acquisition of his new car. He also attributed his irritation to the traffic ticket, while his anger was due to his vehicle being repossessed. By understanding suffering arises from within us, we can remove suffering from our lives. Our suffering arises from our thoughts, words, and actions. It is then experienced by way of our negative emotions.

Third Noble Truth

The Third Noble Truth addresses the cessation of suffering by removing its cause, which is karma and negative emotion. The way to remove karma and negative emotions is to substitute those thoughts, words, and actions that do not create happiness for ourselves and others with those that do. This requires following an ongoing process of self-discipline. Ultimately, complete freedom from suffering requires that we break through the illusions that we have of ourselves and discover the truth of who we are, which is Anatta. The way to do this is the subject of the Fourth Noble Truth; it is discussed in the next chapter.

Chapter 9: The Eightfold Path

The Fourth Noble Truth offers guidance on how to remove suffering from our lives, which involves following the eight paths of discipline, which is why it is known as the Eightfold Path. The Eightfold Path serves to cultivate ethical conduct, mental discipline, and wisdom. The eight paths that it is comprised of include: Correct concentration, correct mindfulness, correct intention, right view, correct speech, correct action, correct livelihood, and correct effort.

Correct Concentration

To change our karma and emotions, we need to not only be aware of them, but we need to be able to transcend them. This requires a stable mind. For most of us, our minds are over-represented by negative thoughts and emotions. Without correct concentration, our minds will remain unstable.

Meditation is used to calm the mind and allows one to establish a stable mind that is grounded in stillness.

Correct Mindfulness

If correct concentration is acquired through mediation, then it is important to meditate correctly. Learning to meditate correctly requires mindfulness. Correct mindfulness is the ability to clearly perceive what is occurring while we are meditating. This would include things like the arising of thoughts and sensations.

When being mindful, one is aware of thoughts, perceptions, and sensations as they arise and fade into consciousness. Without mindfulness, one will not discern the subtle thoughts that prevent one from progressing into deeper meditation.

With practice, mindfulness is carried over from meditation into daily life. No longer caught up in thought, one becomes established in the present moment.

Correct Intention

In Buddhism, there are three kinds of correct intentions:

Intention of Renunciation: As attachment creates suffering, learning to renunciate from material goods is necessary. This does not mean we do not enjoy material goods; instead, we do not become attached to them.

Intention of Goodwill: We often make decisions in life that are ultimately based on our self-interest. Practicing goodwill causes us to focus on creating happiness and value for others. Ultimately, the intention for goodwill is a renunciation of an ego-centered mind.

Intention of Harmlessness: Related to the Intention of Goodwill, the Intention of Harmless calls for us to not create suffering for other beings, including ourselves.

Right View

Each Buddhist sect has its own interpretation or description of what constitutes the highest view of reality. In other words, what is the nature of ultimate reality? Based on this, one who practices Buddhism strives to cultivate the ability to discern that reality. When we can do this, we have the right view. What this means is that, during meditation and daily life, one can distinguish between the fabrications of the mind and ultimate reality.

Correct Action

While the previous paths dealt with the mind, correct action refers to how we conduct ourselves in our daily lives. Correct action is conduct that results in benefiting both others and ourselves. As the seed of all actions is thought, holding correct intentions leads to correct action.

Correct Speech

Our speech has tremendous power to influence others. It can cause others to change their thinking, move hearts, or create suffering. To have correct speech is to be aware of how our speech affects others and to ensure that our words benefit them. Speech that causes harm to others is the antithesis of correct speech, as is idle speech.

Idle speech is a mindless chit chat that offers no value to whom it is directed to. Correct speech can be developed by making it a practice to recite Buddhist scripture, mantras, and prayers.

Correct Livelihood

Correct livelihood simply means that we choose vocations or careers that do not cause harm to others or the Earth. We want to choose work that directly or indirectly benefits others.

Correct Effort

None of the previous seven paths can be achieved without consistent effort. They all require consistent effort to improve. There is no such thing as attaining them overnight or through prayer. It is for this reason that the previous seven paths rely on the eighth path, correct effort.

It is important to note, however, that the word

"effort" has a different meaning in Buddhism than the meaning that we commonly associate it with. In the English language, "effort" is often associated with things like drudgery or being a chore.

In Buddhism, the meaning of effort is associated with enthusiasm and joy. The mark of effort in Buddhism is an effort that is stable and consistent. It is this kind of effort that is needed to be successful with any of the previous seven paths.

The Eightfold Path can be simplified by creating categories for the individual paths:

Cultivating Ethical Conduct: This category would include correct speech, correct action, correct livelihood, and correct effort.

Mental Discipline: In this category, we would find correct view, correct concentration, and correct mindfulness.

The reason why the Eightfold Path leads to enlightenment is that, as stated earlier, karma is created by thoughts, words, and actions. Following the Eightfold Path, we can live our lives in a way that is the antithesis of how we lived in the past, which is the source of our karma. Following the Eightfold Path breaks one's karmic cycle by cultivating the thoughts, words, and deeds that lead to wisdom and enlightenment. What results from ethical conduct and mental discipline is wisdom.

Chapter 10: The Five Aggregates

The five aggregates are a core teaching in Buddhism that explains cognition and how personal experience is created. Additionally, they help enhance understanding of other teachings such as Anatta (non-self) and attachments [33]. These five aggregates collaborate to form a human being. The five aggregates are form, sensation, perception, mental formation, and consciousness.

Form

The first aggregate, form, refers to the physicality that we experience in the world. When we experience anything that appears to be solid or have shape, this is the first aggregate. The first aggregate is also known as Rupa. Our bodies are equipped with five sense organs: Ears, eyes, nose, and tongue. As an extension of these, Rupta also includes the objects of the sense organs, which would consist of sight, smell, taste, and sound [34].

Sensations

The second of the five aggregates, sensation, refers to the three kinds of feelings or sensations: Pleasant, unpleasant, and indifferent. In other words, we experience sensations that are pleasurable, unpleasant, or neutral.

Perception

Perception is the process by which a given experience is conceptualized within our minds. This conceptualization creates our experience of reality. We will explain this in more detail later in this section.

Mental Formation

The fourth aggregate is mental formation. This aggregate is the cumulative conditioned responses to the objects of experience. It is cumulative because it stores the conditioned responses from all past lives to the present moment.

Imagine a child who touches a hot stove, resulting in them burning themselves. The child knows in the future that stoves are hot and cause pain. Because of this, the child avoids stoves in the future. The child's avoidance is a conditioned response, and the object of experience is the stove. The fourth aggregate is a storehouse for all conditioned responses from the beginningless past up to the present moment. What this means is that not all of your conditioned responses were created in this lifetime. Some of them were carried over from previous lives.

Consciousness

The fifth aggregate is consciousness, and it is the most fundamental of all the aggregates. All the other aggregates are contained within consciousness. Without consciousness, there can be no experience.

When the child touched the stove, three elements were involved in creating the child's experience. The first two elements were the body and the stove. However, the body and the object alone cannot create experience.

The third element, consciousness, becomes associated with the body and object. It is the association of these three elements that create experience. The same is true with seeing. If you look at a rose, your eyes and the visible object, the rose, cannot produce an experience without the existence of consciousness. All sensory organs and their objects rely on consciousness for the creation of experience.

When consciousness becomes associated with the sensory organs (first three aggregates) and their objects, consciousness takes on different forms. These forms are: Eye-consciousness, ear-consciousness, nose-consciousness, tongue-consciousness, body-consciousness, and mind-consciousness [35]. In Buddhism, the mind is considered one of the sense organs [33].

There is only one consciousness; however, it expresses itself as the localized consciousness of the various sense organs.

The Creation Of Experience

The following scenarios illustrate the role of the five aggregates in creating experience. Imagine you are walking in the woods when your eyes (the aggregate of form) spot a visible object, a rattlesnake (which is also the aggregate of form). At that moment, the aggregate of consciousness becomes aware of the object, though the object remains unidentified [34].

The aggregate of perception identifies the object as a rattlesnake. Recognizing this, you become fearful (the aggregate of feeling). You respond to the rattlesnake by walking around it (The aggregate of mental formation).

In another scenario, you are listening to music. Your ears (the aggregate of form) connect with the sound of the music (the aggregate of form). The aggregate of consciousness becomes aware of sound. In turn, the sound is recognized as music by the aggregate of perception. Finally, an emotional response to the music is created by the aggregate of feeling. The aggregate of mental formation determines how you react to the music, be it singing, dancing to it, or changing to a new song.

The Impermanence Of Experience

The five aggregates are not objects; instead, they are processes. As with everything else in life, their nature is that of impermanence also. The five aggregates are continually changing.

The body, the aggregate of form, changes with the advent of health and aging. The aggregate of feelings changes when we start having positive feelings toward things that we once were disinterested in, or Visa Versa. How we perceive is subject to change. What may appear to be a snake in a semi-lit room turns out to be a rope when the lights are turned on. The aggregate of mental formation changes as demonstrated by us quitting of old habits and adopting new ones.

The Five Aggregates And Attachment

Our attachment to mind and body is ultimately the

attachment to the experiences created by the five aggregates. We continually refer to ourselves as "I":

"I see a beautiful sunset."

"I love the smell of lavender."

"I feel sad."

"I hear an alarm."

"I am having bad thoughts."

However, we are not the five aggregates. The essence of who we are is the fifth aggregate; who we are fundamentally is consciousness. When the five aggregates come together, a human being is formed. When the five aggregates are no longer held together by consciousness, only consciousness remains.

What we refer to as death is the liberation of consciousness from the other aggregates. However, one does not have to wait for death for his kind of liberation. One can enjoy it while living. This is the purpose of Buddhist practice.

Chapter 11: The Twelve Links Of Dependent Origination

The Buddhist scholar and saint, Lama Tsongkhapa, once stated that the Twelve Links of Dependent Origination was the most profound of all the Buddha's teachings. The Buddha himself was reported to have said that, on the day that he reached enlightenment, he awoke to the Twelve Links of Dependent Origination [36].

The Buddha believed this principle most clearly depicts how living beings end up getting trapped in the endless cycle of birth and death. The Buddha even went on to say that none of his teachings could be fully understood without a clear understanding of this principle [36].

The 12 Links of Dependent Origin incorporate elements of other core Buddhist principles, including the Four Noble Truths, the Five Aggregates, and karma. Because of this, the 12 Links of Dependent Origin can be viewed as a synthesis of the different teachings from the Buddha. In doing so, it also provides a deeper understanding of the other teachings.

Samsara is a Buddhist term that refers to the cycle of birth and death. All living beings are trapped in this cycle. We remain caught in this cycle because of the karma that we create for ourselves.

Imagine the cycle of birth and death to be a wheel. The 12 links can be imagined as sections of that wheel. In the course of our lives, we pass through each section of the wheel. Because we do not understand this cycle, we continue to pass through the sections lifetime after lifetime.

By understanding this cycle, we can make changes in our lives and eventually escape this cycle. As long as we are caught in this cycle, we will experience suffering. When we come to understand this cycle (within our being, not just intellectually), we will become free of suffering.

Because of the complexity of the 12 Links of Dependent Origination, we will start first by reviewing each of the links. We will then look at how the links work together to shape the course of our lives. The 12 links are ignorance, mental formations, consciousness, name and form, contact, feelings, craving, grasping, becoming, birth, and aging/death.

Overview Of The 12 Links

Ignorance

The first link, ignorance, refers to not knowing our true nature, which is Buddhahood or enlightenment. This confusion occurs when the mind creates a sense of separation between us and the object that it is discerning.

In the section on the five aggregates, it was mentioned that consciousness takes on different forms and that they correspond to the sense organs. We will use eye-consciousness as an example.

When the eye makes contact with an object, eye-consciousness becomes associated with the object. Besides becoming associated with the object, eye-consciousness also becomes associated with the mental factor of ignorance. These combined associations become imprinted in the larger consciousness.

Imagine that you enter a room that is poorly lit when you see what appears to be a snake (an object) on the floor. You then turn on the lights and see that it is not a snake but a rope.

Before the lights were turned on, eye-consciousness

became associated with the object. This resulted in you having the experience of seeing the object. The mental factor of ignorance became associated with the eye-consciousness and the object. This led you to believe that you saw a snake. This conclusion became imprinted in your consciousness.

When you turned on the light, you saw the true nature of the object, that is was a rope. The difference between the two experiences was the presence or absence of ignorance. The previous scenario is played out in our daily lives. Our experience is based on ignorance.

We experience ourselves as a physical body with a mind. Further, we experience ourselves as being a unique entity that is separate from the rest of life. This view is like seeing the snake in the dark room. The enlightened one can be compared to turning on the lights and finding out that it is a rope. Instead of a rope, we perceive our true nature.

It is for the above reasons that ignorance is the fundamental cause of all of our sufferings. Whether it is our insecurities, disharmony between two individuals, or global warfare, all of these sufferings arise from the same place, our ignorance toward ourselves and others.

Mental Formation

The second link is mental formation, which is a fancy word for action. The misconceptions that we make (like mistaking the rope for a snake) results in actions. Because these actions are made from ignorance, we do not take wise actions. It is our ill-informed actions that create karma.

The strength of our actions will determine the power of the karmic energy that results from it. If I have an argument with someone, but I am generally easy-going, my actions (the arguing) will be less of a karmic force than it would be if I am habitually argumentative.

When I was first introduced to Buddhism, I read my prayer book and meditate only occasionally. During my last 20 years of Buddhist practice, I have read my prayer book and meditated daily. In my pre-Buddhist days, the positive karmic energy that I generated was minimal compared to the karmic energy that I generate today.

Whether positive or negative, our habitual ways of behaving and thinking become deeply ingrained in our consciousness and create our karma. (This a simplified statement. There are different levels of consciousness. Imprinting affects only certain layers of consciousness. This will be further discussed in the next section).

Consciousness

Consciousness is the 3rd link. When discussing consciousness, in the context of the 12 links of dependent origination, we are talking about a specific layer of consciousness. This layer is rarely considered outside of Buddhism. Before discussing this layer, we will first discuss the Buddhist model of consciousness, known as the nine consciousness [38].

The first five layers of consciousness are associated with the sense organs, which was explained under the section of the Five Aggregates. The first five layers are:

- Sight consciousness
- Hearing consciousness
- Smell consciousness
- Taste consciousness
- Touch consciousness

These conscious layers perceive information about

the world. This information is received by the conscious layer below it, the sixth consciousness. The six consciousness integrates the information from the first five layers into a coherent image. It is from this image that the six consciousness formulate a response. It is at the level of the sixth consciousness that most of us operate from as we conduct our daily activities. This is also the layer where dreaming, memory, and thoughts occur.

Below the sixth consciousness is the seventh consciousness. It differs from the previous six layers in that it has an inward orientation, whereas the previous six layers are oriented toward the outer world. The seventh consciousness is where our basic sense of identity arises from as well as our sense of morality. It is also the layer where our sense of being a separate and unique entity originates from.

The next layer down is the eighth consciousness, also known as the *Alaya* consciousness. The Alaya consciousness is the storehouse of karma. This includes karma from all of our past lives and our current one.

The eight consciousness plays a vital role in the *12 links of dependent origination*. When karmic energy is generated from our actions, it leaves its imprint on the eight consciousness. The karmic energy contained within the eighth consciousness flows into the first seven layers, influencing their functioning.

If I have strong karmic energy, created by my mistrust of others, it will flow from the Alaya consciousness and leave its stain on all the layers above it. At the seventh layer of consciousness, it will lead me to believe that I am a person who has trust issues.

At the sixth layer, it will determine what actions I need to take when meeting someone. At the first five layers, what I see, what I hear, and what I feel about the other person will pass through a lens, a lens whose focus is on why people cannot be trusted.

At a more profound level, it is the Alaya consciousness that reincarnates upon our death. The first seven consciousness will fade away, but the Alaya consciousness will retain our karma and reappear when we are reborn. During reincarnation, it is not a question of what we come back as. Instead, it is about our past karma returning in a new life form.

The ninth layer of consciousness, the deepest layer, is pure consciousness. This layer is free of karma. No experience can leave an imprint on it. At this level, even thought is absent. This layer represents our authentic nature; this is our Buddha nature.

When we realize our Buddha nature, it will purify all the layers above it. When this happens, the eight remaining layers will function at their highest level.

What results from this is equanimity, bliss, and wisdom. Without exception, all of the Buddha's teachings are directed toward the realization of the ninth consciousness.

Name And Form

Name and form, the fourth link, can be thought of as mind and body. "Name" refers to the mind. The mind is labeled as such because it engages objects through discrimination. The mind operates through duality; it is always comparing objects (Example: "This is this" and "that is that").

In Buddhism, birth does refer to the delivery of the baby; rather, it indicates the stage before the development of the sense organs in the fetus. It is at this stage that name and form are indicated [37].

Six Sense Spheres

The fifth link is the sense spheres, which refers to when the fetus develops sensory organs. Because the sense organs are present, the formation of new karma begins here. We will discuss the six sense spheres in more detail later in this chapter.

Contact

The sixth link, contact, refers to when a sense organ meets an object. An example of contact would be when you see an apple or taste one. In the case of the sense spheres, the fetus makes contact with the emotional and physiological activity of the mother.

Feeling

Feelings, the seventh link, arise from contact with an object. Feelings are classified as being pleasurable, neutral, and unpleasant.

Craving

The eighth link is craving. Craving is a form of attachment. There are three forms of craving: Craving for pleasure, craving for annihilation, and craving for existence.

Craving for pleasure is the attachment to a pleasurable sensation. We crave to prolong or repeat a pleasurable sensation. An example would be having eaten a particular food in the past; we desire to have that food again.

Craving for annihilation is the craving to end the experience of suffering. While this would seem to be a normal desire, it becomes problematic when our thoughts for ending our suffering involve avoiding it or destroying it. An example of this would be that we recall an unpleasant memory, so we distract ourselves by getting involved with something that we find more enjoyable.

The reason why Buddhism does not consider this to be a wise decision is that we are creating attachments, attachments to the more pleasurable activity and attachment to the avoidance of the unpleasurable experience.

Craving for existence has to do with experiences of going into deep meditation. When in deep meditation, one experiences a peaceful but neutral sensation. One can crave to remain in this experience. Even this is a form of attachment.

Grasping

The ninth link is grasping. Grasping is another version of attachment; however, it differs from craving. While cravings condition karmic energy, grasping brings karmic energy to its full expression. This manifestation occurs at the time of our death and leads to our next rebirth. In other words, grasping ensures that our current karma follows us to our next incarnation.

At the end of our lives, we may come to realize that those things that we relied on to give us a sense of self have not fulfilled their purpose. Whether it is our relationships, our fortunes, or our possessions, we will realize that there is still an emptiness that remains unfilled. The things that we relied on to fill our emptiness will continue to drive us in our next lifetime.

Becoming

Becoming, the tenth link, is the actualization of karma. It is the bridge between mental formation and consciousness. Our most potent karmic energy becomes the last experience in our life. Upon us passing away, our karma continues into the next lifetime.

Imagine that you took the life of another person. The

memory of that event will permeate your consciousness at the time of your death. The emotions associated with that event, such as anger, will leave a deep imprint in the Alaya consciousness and will be carried over to your next lifetime.

Birth

As indicated before, birth, the eleventh link, occurs at conception. The mind is not the product of birth but instead is carried over to the embryo from the previous life. In other words, birth is the continuation of the mind and karma. It is for this reason that suffering begins at birth.

Aging And Death

Aging and death are combined in the twelfth link because of their unique relationship. In Buddhism, aging refers to the continuous change that begins at the time of conception. Death, on the other hand, can occur at any time during the life of the organism.

Dependent Origination

As its name implies, dependent origination refers to the fact that everything that exists depends on something else, from which it originates. The 12 links can be classified into three groups: Impelling cause, actualization causes, and results. Impelling causes and actualization causes combine to explain the origin of suffering. Results speak to the truth of suffering.

Impelling Causes

Impelling causes are those links that set into motion the creation of suffering. Impelling causes include ignorance, mental formation, and consciousness. Ignorance leads to mental formation, which creates karma (action). In turn, action leaves an imprint on consciousness.

Actualization Causes

Actualization causes are those links that lead to suffering be actualized. They include cravings, grasping, and becoming. The karmic imprint on consciousness becomes manifested as craving, while cravings lead to grasping. At the time of death, karmic energy returns to consciousness, which is what is known as becoming.

Result

Result causes are the links that are the truth of suffering. They include name and form, six sense spheres, contact, feeling, birth, and aging and death. At death, the continuation of the mind is carried over to the next birth, which leads to name and form. At the moment of birth, aging and death begin.

As the development of the fetus continues, the six

sense-spheres develop. When the six sense-spheres perceive an object, contact occurs, which results in feelings. The cycle then repeats itself. Feelings lead to cravings and grasping, while grasping eventually leads to becoming, and so on. It is through this cycle that suffering is transmitted from lifetime to lifetime.

Through the 12 links of dependent origin, we create karma. Though the physical body will vanish after our death, the Alaya consciousness, where our karmic energy is stored, will continue on and manifest again at the time of rebirth. It is only when we can recognize our true nature that we can stop the cycle of birth and death. Buddhist practice provides the tools to accomplish this.

Chapter 12: The Seven Factors

As indicated before, Buddhism does not rely on faith. Instead, Buddhism is based on exerting one's self in practice and experiencing what the Buddha spoke of. We have so far discussed the core teachings of the Buddha, such as the Four Noble Truths, the Eightfold Paths, the Five Aggregates, and the 12-Links of Dependent Origin.

Regardless of the teaching, certain mental qualities need to be developed to understand the teaching truly. Interestingly, the cultivating of these qualities within themselves lead to the same insights as the teachings themselves. The qualities that I speak of are known as the Seven Factors.

Ultimately, the thing that every person wants is to be happy. In the Western world, the traditional approach to happiness has been to pursue it in the form of relationships, profession, social standing, or financial wealth. Others seek a mental health professional. It is not uncommon for a therapist to work with a client for months, even years, focusing on their pathology.

In Buddhism, the focus is to uncover the mind's potentials for creating happiness. These potentials are referred to as the Seven Factors. They are the mental qualities that the Buddha considered to be necessary for correct spiritual practice. These qualities are mindfulness, investigation, effort, joy, tranquility, concentration, and equanimity.

Mindfulness

Mindfulness is the cultivating of awareness to the nature of reality. As previously stated, ignorance is the cause of suffering. We experience only a small sliver of reality. The reason for this is that most of us are preoccupied with our thoughts.

Our thoughts throw a veil on reality by redirecting our attention to the past or the future. The past is our memories, and the future is our anticipations. However, neither memories or anticipation reflect true reality; instead, they are mental constructs. To understand reality, one must be aware of the present moment. It is about being aware of one's thoughts, one's emotions, the sensations in the body, and what is occurring around us. Practicing mindfulness cultivates this kind of knowing.

Being mindful is particularly important in mediation as it allows us to be aware of any intrusive thoughts without getting caught up in them. Only when one develops such awareness can the deeper levels of meditation be reached.

Investigation

The dharma refers to the laws of life, and the purpose of Buddhism is to develop an intimate understanding of the dharma. To understand anything requires research. The Buddha once famously said: "Believe nothing no matter where you read it or who said it unless it agrees with your common sense and observation." [3]

What the Buddha meant by this was that it is our job to investigate his teachings for ourselves and then evaluate their truthfulness. He did not want us to accept his words on face value. Understanding the true nature of ourselves and of reality requires our personal investigation. Buddhist teachings function to point the direction of our inquiry.

Diligence

Like any endeavor, Buddhist practice takes diligence. Our lives are filled with distractions. It takes diligence to meditate each day, to develop mindfulness, and to challenge our habits. Like any of the other seven factors, this quality can also be cultivated.

Joy

A sense of joy for exploring the infinite potential of our lives and the nature of reality is essential. Without a sense of joy, what will motivate us to continue practicing? If we do not keep practicing, we will not be able to transcend the ignorance created by the mind.

While a sense of joy for practicing Buddhism is needed, this does not mean one must have a sense of joy in the beginning. One who approaches Buddhist practice with a sense of determination will uncover the feelings of joy naturally. The reason for this is that it is the natural state of the mind to be joyous. The reason why most of us do not feel joyous is that we allow our attention to be monopolized by our minds and our ignorance.

Tranquility

To be tranquil is to relax, and it is important to relax if one is to gain benefit from Buddhist practice. Tranquility is important because it allows us to experience the deeper potentials of the mind, which are obscured when we are frustrated, anxious, or preoccupied with our thoughts. As with any of the seven factors, tranquility can be cultivated through Buddhist practice.

Concentration

I want you to try something. Sit down, allow yourself to relax, and close your eyes. Place your attention on your breath. Experience the sensations that you feel as your breath enters and leaves your body. When you are focusing on your breath, you are demonstrating concentration.

While concentrating on your breath, you may feel

yourself becoming more relaxed. The reason for this is because you can only focus on one thing at a time. Since your breathing is monopolizing your attention, your thoughts are being deprived of it. This is what creates a disciplined mind, learning to focus your concentration.

Equanimity

Of all the seven factors, equanimity is one of the most profound. It is normal for us to experience positive feelings when things go well and negative feelings when we experience loss. It is on this emotional roller coaster that most of us ride for the duration of our lives. This emotional ride is the result of us identifying with the illusions of who we think we are as opposed to our deeper truth.

The truth of who you are transcends any thought, perception, or sensation that you may experience. In fact, the truth of who you are transcends experience itself. There is nothing in life that can create joy or disturbance within you. Instead, it is our illusionary sense of self that projects these emotions on to our experience.

Your thoughts, emotions, perceptions, and sensations are like fish swimming in the ocean, and you are the ocean. The ocean allows fish to swim freely while being untouched by their movements. It is like this that your experiences move through the streams of consciousness, of which ultimately you are.

When we are in a state of equanimity, we will not get caught up in our fleeting emotions. Whether our experiences are positive or negative, we will maintain an attitude of complete acceptance. This does not mean that we remain emotionless. Emotions will still appear, but we lose our reactivity toward them.

Chapter 13: The Foundation Of Mindfulness

The foundations of mindfulness, also known as Satipatthana, is a teaching for the establishment of mindfulness. Mindfulness is one of the Buddha's fundamental teachings, and all Buddhist sects observe it.

The Buddha's commentary on mindfulness was as follows:

"Contemplating our experience internally, externally, and both; Contemplating the nature of impermanence: the arising, the passing away, and both the arising and passing away in regard to our experience; Abiding without clinging to anything that enters our realm of experience." [40]

From a Buddhist perspective, mindfulness is about developing awareness both internally and externally.

Internal awareness involves cultivating awareness, so the coming and going of thoughts, perceptions, and sensations can be discerned. External awareness means to be aware of what is happening externally, meaning in our environment. When we can do both simultaneously, without judging or personalizing our experiences, we are practicing mindfulness.

The four foundations provide a systematic approach to mindfulness practice. This approach consists of a series of steps or foundations. The four foundations are mindfulness of the body, mindfulness of feelings, mindfulness of the mind, and mindfulness of the dharma.

Mindfulness Of The Body

To have mindfulness of the body is to be aware of the body. When practicing mindfulness of the body, we are aware of it as an object. We learn to not view it as "my body." Instead, it becomes just another object in our experience. Our experience of the body is not personalized.

While being mindful of the body, one becomes aware of the experiences of the body as they present themselves. There is a knowing of the movement of breath, the positioning of the body, how the body moves, as well as of its other qualities.

Mindfulness Of Feelings

Just as with the body, feelings can also be the object of mindfulness. To be mindful of feelings is to be aware of them as they arise within us as well as their departure from our awareness. As with all mindful practices, the goal is to be aware of them without labeling them or forming judgments about them.

Further, being mindful of feelings means not to personalize them. It is enough to be aware of their existence.

It is not uncommon to experience feelings that we are uncomfortable with. Because we do not want to experience certain feelings, we suppressed them. During the practice of mindfulness, these feelings may appear.

Since feelings are forms of energy, suppressing them leads to them expressing themselves in ways that do not serve us. We are not our feelings; we are the ones that are aware of them. Should such feelings arise during mindfulness practice, consider this to be a benefit. By acknowledging them, they will fade away.

Mindfulness Of Mind

Concerning mindfulness of the mind, what is referred to as "mind" is different from our normal understanding of it. In this case, "mind" (known as

Citta) refers to consciousness. This consciousness is free of thoughts; however, it is not refined to the level of pure consciousness. Instead, this mind consists of our different mental states. Just as with thoughts, our mental states also appear and disappear within consciousness.

Being mindful of the mind is to be aware of the coming and going of mental states such as sleepiness, alertness, being disoriented, clarity, and so on. When being mindful of the mind, one understands that all mental states are transitory and are insubstantial.

Mindfulness Of The Dharma

The final foundation is the mindfulness of Dharma. The word "Dharma" has a variety of meanings. Dharma could refer to the natural intelligence of the universe, the laws of nature, the manifestations of reality, or the Buddha's teachings.

In being mindful of the dharma, what is being referred to is being mindful of mental objects. Everything we experience in the world is a mental object. As it was discussed in the 12-links to dependent origination, everything that we experience is experienced as an imprint within consciousness.

Our experience of the world is a mental representation within our consciousness. These representations are impermanent, lack an absolute self, and are highly conditioned. As previously explained in the 12-links of dependent origin, the meaning that we give to experience, along with how we react to that experience, becomes ingrained in our consciousness. Experience is created by consciousness being colored by the meaning and response that we give to a situation.

Given the involvement of all these elements in the creation of our experiences, there is an acknowledgment of the inter-existence of experience.

Applying What You Have Learned: Mindfulness Exercises

The following are three beginner's exercises in mindfulness:

Mindfulness Of Walking

Before starting this exercise, designate a short distance (approximately ten feet) in which you will practice mindful walking. As you get more comfortable with this exercise, you can extend the distance.

1. With your route marked out, walk at a relaxed pace, the distance of your path. As you walk, place your attention on the sensations that you experience as the soles of your feet make contact

with the ground. Experience the sensations of taking a step forward and of your feet returning to the ground.

2. As you become more skillful in focusing on the sensations of walking, you can extend your awareness to what is happening in your environment. Listen to the sound of birds singing, the wind blowing, the sound of cars, or people talking. As always in mindful practice, do not judge, analyze, or evaluate anything that you experience. Your only job is to be aware.

Mindfulness In Observing

1. Sit down and make yourself comfortable.
2. Close your eyes and focus on your breath, allowing yourself to become relaxed.
3. Now look around at your surroundings. What is the quality of your experience as you view your environment? You may wish to rate your experience from 1-10, with ten being the highest.

4. Now close your eyes and relax. I want you to imagine that you are an alien from another planet and that you have been sent down to Earth to observe what it is like here. You do not know anything about this planet. You have no words to describe your experience, and you have no concepts for what you are experiencing. All that you have is your immediate and direct experience.

5. Keeping all of this in mind, open your eyes and observe your surroundings again. You can scan your environment or focus on a particular object that you find interesting. Take your time to observe.

6. When you are ready, rate your experience of observing again. Was there a difference from the first time you observed? What were those differences? Was there a greater freshness to your observation?

If you could not detect a difference, that is okay. Continue to practice this technique until you can detect a difference in the quality of your experience when observing.

Mindfulness Of The Sensations Of The Body

1. Close your eyes and place your attention on your breath during inhalation and exhalation. Place your attention on your breathing. Feel it as it courses through your body.

2. Now place your attention on the sensations of the body. Place your attention on any sensation of the body that you experience. Do you feel a tingling in your hands or feet? Do you feel a tension in your back, shoulders, or face? Do you feel the weight of your body? Can you detect the pressure on your buttocks from the chair or the ground that you are sitting on?

Allow yourself to experience the sensations of the body without any judgment, even the ones that may feel unpleasant. There are no good or bad sensations. Good and bad, pleasant and unpleasant, these are value judgments that exist solely in mind. The same thing is true with perceptions, sounds, and thoughts.

This is the end of this meditation. Continue to meditate on the body for as long as you wish.

Chapter 14: The Six Paramitas

The Six Paramitas are the path of the Bodhisattva. In Sanskrit, the word paramita can be translated as "Crossing over to the other shore." Other definitions include "perfection" or "reaching beyond limitations." [42]

By practicing the six paramitas, we can cross the ocean of suffering and land on the shores of Nirvana. In other words, we travel from the storms of our delusional minds to a place of equanimity and freedom.

The six paramitas can be thought of as the standards of excellence for the heart and mind. The capacity to meet these standards is innate within us all. For this reason, we can consider the six paramitas as seeds. If attended to, these seeds will eventually sprout into Buddhahood. The way these seeds mature is through the daily practice of being loving, compassionate, and wise in the way we live our lives.

Perfection Of Giving (Dana Paramita)

The first paramita is the perfection of giving. It is giving without any attachments or expectations. Often, our giving is not pure as our actions may be tainted by secondary motives. These motives include having expectations when giving, feeling obligated to give, the hope of receiving recognition, or giving due to a sense of guilt.

We practice the first paramita by giving of our attention, compassion, time, or our resources. Additionally, we do not qualify as to who is deserving of our giving . To truly follow the first paramita, we are to enhance the welfare of all living beings. What this means is that our giving should be unconditional.

At a deeper level, the power behind the first paramita is not in our giving or what we give. Instead, its potency is in developing concern for others. Ultimately, the real power behind the first paramita is the dissolving of the egoic mind, the greatest obstacle to experiencing our enlightened nature.

Carrying on the practice of the first paramita can be made easier if we remember that everything in life is impermanent. Our bodies and possessions will all fade away eventually. With this recognition, we should live a daily philosophy of maximizing the use of our minds, bodies, and possessions in order to serve other sentient beings.

The ultimate gift that we can give to others is to share the dharma with others. However, we must do so with caution. We should do so only with those who express an interest in hearing it as opposed to trying to convert others. By practicing the first paramita, we are gradually weakening the illnesses of the mind, which includes possessiveness, miserliness, and greed.

The Perfection Of Ethics (Sila Paramita)

The second paramita, the perfection of ethics, involves the quality of our personal conduct. It includes the qualities of morality, ethical behavior, personal integrity, honor, discipline, and harmlessness.

Broadly speaking, this is the paramita for cultivating love and compassion. It also involves the developing of virtuous thinking, speech, and action. By accomplishing this, we progress in our ability to meditate and reach higher realizations.

The paramita of ethics prevents us from engaging in behavior that is harmful to others. We learn to abstain from killing, sexual misconduct, stealing, harmful or divisive speech, greed, wrong views, or malice.

Far from being restrictive to our lives, the second paramita leads to greater happiness, freedom, and security. These qualities become our internal compass, allowing us to move in the direction of real freedom.

Living by the paramita of perfect ethics means that we no longer have to question ourselves as to whether we are doing the right thing. Additionally, we remain true to ourselves as we are not susceptible to the influences of others. Because of this, we cease to create suffering in our lives.

We benefit by being able to enjoy greater confidence and happiness as we become free of guilt or remorse. Additionally, our lives become more vibrant because we have nothing to conceal from others. The paramita supports the first paramita by enabling us to magnify the results of our generosity.

The Perfection Of Patient Endurance (Kshanti Paramita)

The perfection of patient endurance, the third paramita, is characterized by advanced levels of patience, forbearance, acceptance, and tolerance.

Patient endurance fortifies our minds, giving us the ability to face the challenges of life with unshakable composure and tranquility.

When others do us wrong, we are able to respond back to them in a manner that is devoid of emotional reactivity, resentment, or retaliation. We understand that they are operating from ignorance, allowing us to respond back to them with compassion.

By observing this paramita, we develop a life state that is rooted in a security that leaves us unaffected by the praise of others, good fortune, persecution, or hardship. It is not that we become emotionless or not feeling. Instead, we lose our reactivity toward life.

The third paramita creates clarity and a deep understanding of impermanence and karma.

Further, the third paramita plays a vital role in developing our endurance and forbearance to maintain our Buddhist practice. As a bodhisattva, it allows us to see the beauty and goodness in everyone. Because of this, we become more skillful in guiding them through their sufferings [43].

The Perfection Of Effort And Enthusiastic Perseverance (Virya Paramita)

The first three paramitas (generosity, ethics, and

effort) require continuous practice in order to develop. The development of these enlightened qualities requires a determination to constantly exert one's self, despite the inevitable challenges that will arise.

How do we continue to practice, even when we feel discouraged and feel like giving up? The answer to this question is that we must develop supreme effort and perseverance, the fourth paramita [43].

.

The paramita of perfection of effort consists of the qualities of vigor, endurance, diligence, persistent effort, and vitality. The fourth paramita is fueled by the experience of deep compassion for the suffering of other living beings. It is compassion that fuels the persistence of our efforts.

As with the first paramita (generosity), our dedicated efforts to benefit others are to be unconditional and without expectations. The qualities of dedicated service to others, combined with a lack of expectations, elevate our life state and resonates the powers of our Buddha nature. In other words, we are correctly practicing dharma.

Unless we develop the fourth paramita, we will become sidetracked, disillusioned, or frustrated with our practice. When we practice the perfection of effort, we become excited. We experience the kind of perseverance where we excitedly plow forward, regardless of our failures or setbacks.

In this way, the fourth paramita could be referred to as the strengthening of our character and the development of self-reliance. The third paramita also serves us to prepare for the fifth paramita, the perfection of concentration.

The Perfection Of Concentration (Dhyana Paramita)

The perfection of concentration consists of the qualities of supreme mental stability, contemplation, awareness, and meditation. In Buddhism, there is the expression known as "monkey mind. " Our minds are easily distracted and often noisy. It is continuously associating with the thoughts and feelings that are picked up by its radar. It is from the personalization of such mental activity that keeps us trapped in our habitual behaviors.

Most of humanity allows their minds to control them. The perfection of concentration is the practice that turns the tables on this situation and puts us in the driver's seat. Instead of our minds running the show, we take charge of the mind. The mind becomes stabilized through the practices of mindfulness and meditation .

The result of such a mind is that our mental activity

loses its randomness and becomes stabilized. The vacillation of thoughts and emotions is eliminated. In its place, illumination, clarity, and equanimity become its defining qualities. Insights on how to overcome our habitual thinking, perceptions, and actions arise. It is through such insights that we can cast away the mind's illusions. By removing these illusions, profound wisdom, compassion, and joy spontaneously arise.

Success in the other paramitas cannot be made without the practices of concentration and meditation. Only through inner awareness, which concentration and mediation offer, can the other paramitas blossom. It is for this reason this paramita supports all others.

The Perfection Of Wisdom (Prajna Paramita)

The sixth paramita, the perfection of wisdom, refers

to the highest form of wisdom, understanding, and insight. Such wisdom transcends intellectual knowledge or concepts. This degree of wisdom is associated with reconnecting to one's enlightened nature and is not a property of the mind.

From such wisdom, one receives intimate knowledge of the nature of emptiness and the interdependency of all that exists. Because this wisdom is derived from our enlightened nature, it is flawless. There are no questions that it cannot provide insight to. It offers a recognition of the ultimate truth

It is with this wisdom that one can discern the true nature that lies behind all of life. The dualistic perspective that once formed the foundation of our experience gives way to a deep understanding of the oneness of all existence. Further, there is a realization that all manifestations are a projection of this oneness.

There is a realization that oneness exists within diversity and that diversity exists in oneness. In other words, everything that we experience is an expression of our essential self.

The reason why Buddhist teachings place so much emphasis on developing compassion, for working toward the happiness of others, and for giving, is because of oneness. What we do to other sentient beings is what we do to ourselves.

Every experience we have in life is a teachable moment, and the teacher is the experience that we encounter. Experience is a mirror that is being held up to our lives.

Applying What You Have Learned: Meditating On Compassion

The following is an exercise for cultivating greater

compassion.

Compassion

The most fundamental quality that is needed for a healthy relationship is compassion. You may think of love as the most important quality for a relationship; however, love is often experienced as being conditional. In other words, we have a thought that goes like this: "I will love you as long as you________." You can fill-in the blank.

Compassion is unconditional; you feel compassion for another because you are able to connect to their suffering. The following is an exercise for expanding your compassion. This exercise is really a series of sub exercises, with each one creating the foundation for the following one.

Step 1:

I want you to think of a person or animal that you love. When you have identified the subject of this reflection, I want you to think of all the ways that you appreciate them. Experience the feelings and emotions that you have for your subject and fully experience them.

Next, I want you to think of all the hardships and challenges that they have experienced. Think of the sufferings that they have experienced and make their suffering your own. When you have connected with their sufferings, express your love to them, and wish them happiness.

Step 2:

In this next exercise, you are going to repeat what you did in the first exercise; however, this time, you are going to choose a subject that you have neutral feelings for. For example, your subject could be a clerk at the register where you do your shopping or the mail person. Even though you may not know anything about this person, I want you to imagine the sufferings that they may have experienced in their life.

Use your intuition or your imagination but make their suffering as real as you can. Allow yourself to experience their sufferings as your own. When you have connected with their sufferings, express your love to them, and wish them happiness.

Step 3:

In this third exercise, you are going to repeat what you did in the last two exercises, however, using another subject. In this exercise, your subject is going to be someone who you dislike, avoid, or you do not get along with. I want you to think of the sufferings that they have experienced in their life.

As in the previous exercise, you can use your intuition or imagination if you do not know this person's background. Allow yourself to experience their sufferings as your own. When you have connected with their sufferings, express your love to them, and wish them happiness.

Step 4:

This exercise differs from the previous three exercises because you will not be identifying your subject ahead of time. Instead, you will perform this compassion exercise as you go about your day. I want you to notice the people around you as you conduct your daily business.

Take time to imagine the potential sufferings of the people that you see. Allow yourself to experience their sufferings as your own. When you have connected with their sufferings, express your love to them, and wish them happiness.

Step 5:

This is the final exercise, and for many people, the most difficult one. In this exercise, you will be the subject of your reflection. I want you to reflect on the sufferings that you have experienced in your life.

Allow yourself to experience your sufferings fully; do not minimize anything. Get in touch with the pains that you have experienced. When you have connected with your own sufferings, express love to yourself, and wish yourself happiness.

The exercise that you just completed was an exercise in experiencing compassion, and the subject of your compassion began with the ones that are the easiest for you to experience compassion for those whom you love. Each succeeding exercise became more difficult because the subject of your compassion became further removed from you emotionally.

Most people have trouble loving or showing compassion for themselves, which is why you were the subject in the final meditation. The power of your compassion for others is dependent on your ability to have compassion for yourself. When we lack compassion for others, it is because we lack compassion for ourselves; we project our lack of compassion for ourselves on those who are around us. Conversely, when you develop compassion for yourself, you can truly have compassion for others.

Chapter 15: The Eleven Benefits Of Metta

In the Mettanisana Sutta (Sutta can be translated to mean discourse), the Buddha discussed Metta. Metta is a Pali word for having a strong desire for the happiness and welfare of all living beings [44]. The term can also mean loving-kindness, amity, benevolence, friendliness, and goodwill. In its essence, it is an attitude of love that is free of expectations or self-interest. It is a love that is all-embracing. The Buddha taught that there are eleven benefits from practicing Metta [44], which include:

- Improved sleep
- Enjoyable dreams
- Feeling refreshed upon awakening
- Experiencing love from others
- Experiencing love from animals and celestial beings
- Receiving protection from celestial beings
- Receiving protection from external dangers
- Greater radiance

- Improved facial complexion
- An attitude of peace toward death
- Being reborn into happiness

Improved Sleep

The inability to get a good night's sleep is a common problem. While some people have trouble falling asleep, there are others who can fall asleep but are unable to maintain it throughout the night. Others are able to sleep throughout the night but do not feel refreshed upon waking.

Causes for sleep issues can be external or internal. Distractive sounds in the environment would be an example of external causes. Internal causes include distressing thoughts or unpleasant memories.

In order to function properly in our daily responsibilities, an enjoyable night's sleep is needed.

Sleep should refresh us both mentally and physically.

Even if we blame external causes for our sleep issues, the base cause is internal. If this was not correct, then everyone should have difficulty falling asleep with the television on. Obviously, this is not so. There are people who are unable to fall asleep unless the television is on. This is why improved sleep is the first benefit of Metta.

Whether it a distracting sound or troubling thoughts, developing loving-kindness will allow restful sleep to take place as the distracting sounds and troublesome thoughts will not anchor themselves in our consciousness.

Enjoyable Dreams

One cannot have restful sleep if nightmares or unpleasant dreams are experienced. The dreams themselves are not the cause of our interrupted sleep. Instead, it is our feelings that we experience in response to the dreams that cause our sleep to be interrupted.

Negative feelings stimulate the aspect of consciousness known as Vingnganaya-conscious. This results in imaginary based thoughts to be expressed [45].

These thoughts, though illogical and nonsensical, recycle through our minds and lead to confusion upon awakening. Practicing Metta purifies the mind so that we can enjoy our dreams. Further, negative feelings do not arise in response to unpleasant dreams.

Feeling Refreshed Upon Waking

Does this ever happen to you? You wake up after

having a full night's sleep; yet, you hit the snooze button and go back to sleep. Perhaps, you wake up not feeling rested, despite the fact that you slept throughout the night. Such situations are caused by an unharmonious mental state. The third benefit of practicing Metta is that it eliminates unharmonious mental states so that you are able to wake up feeling both clear and refreshed.

Experiencing Love From Others

If we drill down deep enough, we would realize that the thing that everyone is looking for is love. It is not love as a sentimentality but rather a sense of wholeness. We look for love in our life because we want to feel whole.

The pervading quality of consciousness or Buddhahood is wholeness or oneness. To be enlightened is to know the oneness of all things. This is the real meaning of love.

Because our illusory sense of self conceals our Buddhahood, we do not feel whole. It is for this reason that we seek wholeness by pursuing relationships, power or material goods. However, none of these things can ever give us a feeling of wholeness that is lasting.

Because of the impermanent nature of all things, we will eventually experience the loss of wholeness. Conflict within relationships are inevitable, positions of power are only temporary, and all of our material goods and wealth will eventually fade.

When practicing Metta, one develops a profound desire for the happiness of all living beings. Such a one does not seek love in order to feel love. Instead, they are able to focus on the happiness of others because they feel whole, a wholeness that is unshakable.

The fourth benefit is that living beings are drawn to the one who practices Metta. They feel the love of this person and offer their love in return.

Experiencing Love From The Animals And Celestial Beings

The fifth benefit of practicing Metta is experiencing the love of nonhuman beings, which includes celestial beings and animals. In Pali writings, there is mention of spirits, ghosts, and other heavenly beings who were the disciples of the Buddha. These beings give their love to those who practice Metta.

Receiving Protection From Celestial Beings

It is said in Buddhist philosophy that celestial beings are protective of the one who practices Metta the way a parent protects their child. Such protection keeps practitioners of Metta safe from unexpected disasters and potentially troubling situations. The sixth benefit of practicing Metta is that celestial beings guide us along the correct path as we advance toward the future.

Receiving Protection From External Dangers

The seventh benefit from practicing Metta is that we are protected from harm or injuries due to weapons, fire, or poisons. According to one of the Buddha's sermons, if a person attempts to harm a practitioner of Metta, their actions will backfire on them.

Greater Radiance

In the Pali language, there is the term *Thuwatam Chittam Samadhiyati*, which translates to "Mind becomes serene and concentrated easily." When practicing Metta, the mind becomes anger free, which is known as vyadpada [46].

In Buddhism, there are a number of factors that interfere with the achievement of enlightenment. Such factors are known as hindrances. Anger is one of the greatest hindrances. Anger debilitates the mind's ability to concentrate, and a mind that cannot concentrate cannot become serene. The eighth benefit of Metta is a serene mind, and a serene mind leads to radiance.

Improved Facial Complexion

Practicing Metta meditation cleanses the blood and improves blood circulation. This leads to the ninth benefit of Metta meditation: Improved facial complexion.

An Attitude Of Peace Toward Death

The word Dukkha means suffering. Death is one form

of suffering, a suffering that will be experienced by each one of us. Most of us fear death and avoid thinking about it. However, Buddhism has a different view of death.

As discussed earlier, the purpose of Buddhist practice is the attainment of awakening or Nirvana. To reach enlightenment or Nirvana is to become free of the endless cycle of birth and death.

To Buddhists, impending death can be a precious moment in one's practice. When death approaches, many people experience pain or fear. They have difficulty letting go of their attachments. The Buddhist approach is to confront death with mindfulness so that it can be transformed into victory.

By practicing Metta, one can meet death in a manner that is peaceful and conscious. In doing so, the person becomes one with all of life (dharma) while letting go of all attachments. In this way, one escapes the cycle of birth and death. They win the grand prize, a life of unlimited freedom, eternal peace, and blissfulness. This is the tenth benefit of Metta, an attitude of peace toward death.

Being Reborn Into Happiness

In Buddhism and Hinduism, there is a belief in a multi-layer universe, each with its own realm. Brahma Loka is the highest realm a person can reach. Unlike Buddhahood, which is eternal, Brahma Loka is impermanent as it is part of the material world [45].

Arhats are equivalent to apostles in Christianity. They are highly evolved beings who have advanced toward awakening but have fallen short of achieving Buddhahood. A disciple of the Buddha is someone who devotes their life to practicing the Buddha's teachings [45].

If a disciple practices Mette meditation, but fails to reach Arhat status in this lifetime, he or she will reach the realm of Brahma Loka in the following lifetime. At that time, they will no longer be reborn. Instead, they will reach nirvana in the next lifetime. One who masters Metta in this lifetime will enjoy the same kind of profound happiness, which is the twelfth benefit [45].

Findings By Science On The Benefits Of Loving-Kindness Meditation (Mette)

In studying the effects of Metta meditation on the mind and body, researchers found surprising results [47]. The following are some of their findings:

- Improved mood, as demonstrated by an increase in positive emotions and a decrease in negative ones.

- Enhanced sense of being connected socially.

- A decrease in migraines, chronic pain, and PTSD.

- Causes the part of the brain responsible for empathy and emotional processing to be activated.

- Increases the volume of the brain's gray matter.

- Respiratory sinus arrhythmia (RSA) is increased.

- Slows aging by decreasing the length of telomeres, a cellular structure that contains the biological markers for aging.

- Decreases bias toward others as well as self-criticism.

Applying What You Have Learned: Loving-Kindness (Mette) Meditation

The following are the steps to practice Mette mediation. This meditation has three phases to it [45].

Phase 1

1. Begin this meditation by finding a comfortable place to sit down. You can sit in a chair or on the

floor. When sitting, sit in a straight but relaxed manner. You can also lie down but take care not to fall asleep.

2. Start off by placing your attention on your breath. When breathing, breath normally. Take notice of the sensations that you feel as your breath enters your body during inhalation and leaves during exhalation.

3. As you become aware of the bodily sensations created by your breathing, allow your attention to travel to other sensations in your body.

4. When you come across feelings of constriction in your body, place your attention on it. Do not try to change the constrictive feeling. Instead, give it your complete acceptance. Continue to give it your attention until you feel the constrictive feeling loosening up.

5. For the next few minutes, pay attention to the rhythmic flow of your breath. Should distracting thoughts or emotions appear, acknowledge their presence and then return your attention to your breath.

6. Continue observing your breath until you experience your mind growing calm and quiet. Pay attention to any feelings of joy or serenity that you may experience. You want to reach the state where you experience a sense of stillness and mental clarity.

To experience stillness is to sense an aspect of you that does not change and does not get caught up with thoughts, perceptions, or sensations. Mental clarity is to be aware of all these things as they drift in and out of your consciousness.

Phase 2

1. When you have found a state of stillness and mental clarity, ask yourself the following questions. Also, trust the first answer that comes to you.

    Question 1: What would you like to attract into your life that would make your life fulfilling, meaningful, and happy? Your answer can be something material in nature, or it could be something spiritual or intangible.

2. When you have your answer, imagine that it is in your life at this moment. Make the experience of this as vivid as possible in your mind. Pay attention to the feelings that arise as you experience your deepest wishes being actualized.

3. Now that you have identified what you want for your life, and you are experiencing the feelings associated with it, it is time to take this meditation a step deeper. Imagine what else you

would like to have in your life that would expand your happiness even further.

4. When you have identified this, ask yourself how the people or the environment around you could support you in obtaining your wishes. As indicated in the first part of this question, your wishes can be material in nature or nonphysical.

5. Next, ask yourself the following questions:

   Question 2: Ask yourself what kind of person would you like to become? Do you want to become more confident, more relaxed, or more compassionate? What changes would you like to see in yourself? What would be your ideal self? When you think about how you want to be as a person, consider both short and long term changes. When you identify the changes that you want to make, imagine these changes taking place right now!

Question 3: It is important to realize that you, other people, and the environment are interdependent of each other. Each one of us is like a single strand of a spider's web. If one strand is touched, all other strands are affected. All of your actions, and inactions, have an impact on the world. Because of this, the next question to ask yourself is, what would you like to give most to those in your immediate surroundings as well as the world as a whole? You want to think of the kind of legacy that you want to leave behind.

6. When you come up with your answers to this question, visualize yourself engaged in this giving right now! Make it as real as possible! Focus on the feelings that you experience as you see yourself giving to others. As you do so, silently say the following to yourself: *"May I be happy and may I experience the causes of happiness."*

Phase Three

1. As you imagine yourself happily giving back to others, imagine a warm glowing light radiating from your heart. Feel the love, peace, and warmth that is emitted by this light. Experience these feelings grow stronger with each breath. Let them fill your entire being.

2. Ultimately, what you want is to be happy, as do all living beings. The next step is to expand your wish to become happy with all other beings. Take a deep breath and slowly exhale.

3. As you exhale, imagine a rainbow-colored light coming from your heart. Let this light expand until it fills the room that you are in. Should the room be occupied by other people as you meditate, extend your wishes for their happiness by silently saying to yourself: *"May you be happy and may you experience the causes of happiness."*

4. Take another deep breath and then let it out slowly. As you do so, imagine your heat light continue to expand as it fills the entire building and those who are in it. As you do so, silently bless them with the following prayer: *"May you be happy and may you experience the causes of happiness."*

5. Take another deep breath and release it slowly. Now visualize your heart light illuminating the entire neighborhood. Offer each of your neighbors the following thoughts: *"May you be happy and may you experience the causes of happiness."*

6. Take another deep breath and slowly exhale. Imagine your heart light covering your entire city. Silently bless each person in your city with the following thoughts: *"May you be happy and may you experience the causes of happiness."*

7. Continue this mediation by taking another deep breath and slowly let it out. Visualize your heart light bathing your entire country. Offer a silent prayer to the entire population of your country with the following thoughts: *"May you be happy and may you experience the causes of happiness."*

8. Take one more deep breath and exhale slowly. Imagine that you are viewing the planet Earth from outer space. Visualize your heart light encompassing the entire planet. Send every living being on the planet the following prayer: *"May you be happy and may you experience the causes of happiness."*

9. When you have done this, allow yourself to immerse yourself in the feelings of peace or love that you are experiencing. However, do not become attached to any thought, perception, or sensations that you experience. Rather, allow any

experience that you encounter to come and go freely.

Anything that can be experienced is transitory in nature. No experience is immune to change. What is permanent and unchanging is awareness. Just as with space, awareness has no qualities or limitations. No experience can touch awareness. Further, the very existence of experience is dependent upon the existence of awareness.

Awareness, or consciousness, is the essence of who you are. There is only one consciousness, from which all experience manifests. When you pray for your happiness, you are also praying for the happiness of all of existence. When we love others, we are loving ourselves.

10. Now imagine seeing a beam of light before you. In your mind, follow this light as it leads you back to the room where you are meditating. Take one last

final deep breath and silently repeat the following to yourself: *"May I be happy and may I experience the causes of happiness. And may all beings be happy and may they all experience the causes of happiness."*

11. When you are done, slowly open your eyes and allow yourself to remain in your stillness for as long as you desire.

Conclusion

Once there was a poor man who traveled the countryside begging for food and money. He had lived this way for years and had grown to accept his struggles as his destiny. One day as he was resting in a park, he came across an old friend of who he had not seen for years.

The two of them spent the morning talking and catching up on each other's lives. When it was about time to part, the friend invited the poor man home for dinner. The friend was a very successful trader who enjoyed a life of luxury.

When the poor man arrived, the two men spent the evening sharing stories, laughing, eating, and drinking. It got late and the friend saw that the poor man had too much to drink, so he invited him to sleep over.

While the poor man was sleeping, the friend sneaked into his room and took his robe. Within the lining of the robe, he sewed a precious jewel. The next morning, the poor man left the home and went on his way, not knowing what his friend had done.

Years later, the two men crossed paths again. The friend shook his head when he looked at the poor man. It was obvious to him that, since their last meeting, the poor man had continued to live an impoverished life, even though he had in his possession a priceless jewel.

This Buddhist story sums up the entirety of this book. Everything that we could ever want in life exists already within us. Just as with poor man, we are ignorant of the precious jewel that exists within the depths of our lives.

Everything written in this book has been offered with the hopes that it will guide you in discovering this jewel. Buddhism is nothing more than a tool for making this discovery. May the happiness that is inherent to your life shine brightly.

References

1. The Birth and Spread of Buddhism.U.S. History.Org
   http://www.ushistory.org/civ/8d.asp

2. The Buddhist Centre: Buddhism for Today
   https://thebuddhistcentre.com/buddhism

3. Life of the Buddha from Diamond Way Buddhism
   https://www.diamondway-buddhism.org/buddhism/buddha/

4. Theravada: The Way of the Elders. The Pluralism Project Harvard University.
   http://pluralism.org/religions/buddhism/introduction-to-buddhism/theravada-the-way-of-the-elders/

5. What is Theravada Buddhism? Access to Insight. https://www.accesstoinsight.org/theravada.html

6. Introduction to Theravada Buddhism. Learning Religion. https://www.learnreligions.com/theravada-buddhism-450111

7. What is Theravada Buddhism. The Buddhist World   http://www.buddhanet.net/e-learning/buddhistworld/whats-thera.htm

8. Throp, C.L. (2017). Mahayana Buddhism. Ancient History Encyclopedia. https://www.ancient.eu/Mahayana_Buddhism/

9. Theravada and the Mahayana.Buddhanet. http://www.buddhanet.net/e-learning/buddhistworld/schools1.htm

10. Vajrayana Buddhism. Encyclopedia Britannica. https://www.britannica.com/topic/Vajrayana

11. The Vajrayana: The Thunderbolt Vehicle. Buddha.net http://www.buddhanet.net/e-learning/history/b3schvaj.htm

12. Khenpo Karthar Rinpoche (2019). Vajrayana Explained. Lion's Roar.https://www.lionsroar.com/vajrayana-unpacked/

13. Goldberg ,M. (2019) The Root of Mindfulness. Tablet Magazine https://www.tabletmag.com/jewish-life-and-religion/193989/the-roots-of-mindfulness

14. What is "Secular Buddhism"?(2019) Lions Roar. https://www.lionsroar.com/what-is-secular-buddhism/

15. Batchelor, S. (2012). A Secular Buddhist. Tricycle.https://tricycle.org/magazine/secular-buddhist/

16. Buddhism-Major Differences. Buddha.nethttps://www.buddhanet.net/e-learning/snapshot01.htm

17. Caron, M. (n.d.). Buddhism and Hinduism: The Similarities and Differences. Sivana East. https://blog.sivanaspirit.com/buddhism-and-hinduism/

18. Buddhism vs. Islam. Diffen.com https://www.diffen.com/difference/Buddhism_vs_Islam

19. Buddhism vs. Taoism.Diffen.com
https://www.diffen.com/difference/Buddhism_
vs_Taoism

20. Aronson, P. (1999). Reflections of a Jewish
Buddhist. Thubten Chodron.org
https://thubtenchodron.org/1999/06/comparis
on-judaism-buddhism/

21. What Is Mindfulness? Greater Good Science
Center (2016).
http://greatergood.berkeley.edu/topic/mindfuln
ess/definition#how_to_cultivate

22. Weare, K.(n.d.) Mindfulness in Schools Project
https://mindfulnessinschools.org/wp-
content/uploads/2014/10/Evidence-for-
Mindfulness-Impact-on-school-staff.pdf

23. Zedan,F. et al. (2011). Brain Mechanisms Supporting the Modulation of Pain by Mindfulness Meditation. Journal of Neuroscience https://www.jneurosci.org/content/31/14/5540?loc=interstitialskip

24. Posner, M.I. (2012). Imaging attention networks. Science Direct https://www.sciencedirect.com/science/article/abs/pii/S105381191101442X

25. Newburg, A.B. et al. (2013). Meditation and neurodegenerative diseases. Annals of the New York Academy of Sciences https://nyaspubs.onlinelibrary.wiley.com/doi/abs/10.1111/nyas.12187

26. Creswell, J.D. et al. (2012). Mindfulness-Based Stress Reduction training reduces loneliness and pro-inflammatory gene expression in older adults: A small randomized controlled trial.

Science   Direct.
https://www.sciencedirect.com/science/article/
pii/S0889159112001894

27. Muzik, M., et al. (2012). Mindfulness yoga during pregnancy for psychiatrically at-risk women: Preliminary results from a pilot feasibility study. Complementary Therapies in Clinical Practice https://www.sciencedirect.com/science/article/ pii/S1744388112000485

28. Shafer, J. (2016). Neuroplasticity and Clinical Practice: Building Brain Power for Health. Frontiers   in   Psychology. https://www.frontiersin.org/articles/10.3389/fp syg.2016.01118/full

29. Kristeller, J.L., Hallett, C.B. (1999). An Exploratory Study of a Meditation-based Intervention for Binge Eating Disorder. Journal of   Health   Psychology

https://journals.sagepub.com/doi/abs/10.1177/1
35910539900400305

30. Nakamura, Y. et al. (2013). Investigating efficacy of two brief mind–body intervention programs for managing sleep disturbance in cancer survivors: a pilot randomized controlled trial. Journal of Cancer Survivorship. https://link.springer.com/article/10.1007/S1176 4-012-0252-8

31. Anatman. Encyclopedia of Buddhism https://encyclopediaofbuddhism.org/wiki/Anat man

32. McLeod, M. (2018). What are the Four Noble Truths. Lion's Roar. https://www.lionsroar.com/what-are-the-four-noble-truths/

33. The Five Aggregates.Buddhist Door.com http://www.buddhistdoor.com/OldWeb/bdoor/ archive/nutshell/teach11.htm

34. The Five Aggregates.Buddhanet. http://www.buddhanet.net/funbud14.htm

35. The Five Aggregates (2010).Buddhism Teacher. https://buddhismteacher.com/five_aggregates.php

36. The Twelve Links of Interdependent Origination (1980). Lama Yeshe Wisdom Archive https://www.lamayeshe.com/article/twelve-links-interdependent-origination

37. Gache. T. (2019). Personalizing the Twelve Links of Dependent Origination.FPMT.org https://fpmt.org/mandala/online-

features/personalizing-the-twelve-links-of-dependent-origination/

38. The Nine Consciousnesses. SGI. https://www.sgi.org/ru/philosophy/buddhist-concepts/the-nine-consciousnesses.html

39. Bhikkhu, T.H. (2012). Lost in Quotation. Tricycle Magazine: Buddhist Review. https://tricycle.org/magazine/lost-quotation/

40. Goldstein , J. (2013). The Four Foundations of Mindfulness. Lion's Roar. https://www.lionsroar.com/the-four-foundations-of-mindfulness-2/

41. O'Brien,B. (2019). The Seven Factors of Enlightenment: How Enlightenment Manifests. Learn Religion.

https://www.learnreligions.com/the-seven-factors-of-enlightenment-449969

42. The Six Paramitas- Phar-phyin-drug. The Very Venerable 9th Khenchen Thrangu Rinpoche. http://www.rinpoche.com/teachings/paramitas.htm

43. The Six Paramitas. DharmaMind Buddhist Group. http://dharmamind.net/teachings/the-6-parimitas/

44. Benefits of Metta (2019). Mahamegha Media Network. https://mahamegha.lk/2013/09/11/benefits-of-metta/

45. Loving-Kindness Meditation. Zen Awakening. https://zenawakened.com/loving-kindness-meditation/

46. Mettā: Loving-kindness (2009)11th Step Meditation. http://www.11thstepmeditation.org/index.php/meditation-traditions/buddhist-meditations/metta-loving-kindness/

47. Seppaia, E. (2014). 8 Science-Backed Reasons to Try Loving-Kindness Meditation! Psychology Today. https://www.psychologytoday.com/us/blog/feeling-it/201409/18-science-backed-reasons-try-loving-kindness-meditation

Disclaimer

The information contained in this book and its components, is meant to serve as a comprehensive collection of strategies that the author of this book has done research about. Summaries, strategies, tips and tricks are only recommendations by the author, and reading this book will not guarantee that one's results will exactly mirror the author's results.

The author of this book has made all reasonable efforts to provide current and accurate information for the readers of this book. The author and its associates will not be held liable for any unintentional errors or omissions that may be found.

The material in the book may include information by third-parties. Third-party materials comprise of opinions expressed by their owners. As such, the author of this book does not assume responsibility or liability for any third-party material or opinions.

The publication of third-party material does not constitute the author's guarantee of any information, products, services, or opinions contained within third-party material. Use of third-party material does not guarantee that your results will mirror our results. Publication of such third-party material is simply a recommendation and expression of the author's own opinion of that material.

Whether because of the progression of the Internet, or the unforeseen changes in company policy and editorial submission guidelines, what is stated as fact at the time of this writing may become outdated or inapplicable later.

This book is copyright © 2019 by **Sherman Evans** with all rights reserved. It is illegal to redistribute, copy, or create derivative works from this book whole or in parts. No parts of this report may be reproduced or retransmitted in any forms whatsoever without

the written expressed and signed permission from
the author.

191

CPSIA information can be obtained
at www.ICGtesting.com
Printed in the USA
LVHW010023170520
655735LV00006B/433